A Rainbow to Heaven

Hymns, Songs and Chants
by
June Boyce-Tillman

To my good friend Liz

hoping it will motivate your journey

[signature]

Stainer & Bell

First published in 2006 by Stainer & Bell Limited
23 Gruneisen Road, London N3 1DZ

British Library Cataloguing-in-Publication Data
A catalogue record for this book is available from the British Library

ISBN 0 85249 890 X / 978 0 85249 890 3

The photograph of June Boyce-Tillman on the front cover is reproduced
courtesy of TheLightCavalry.com

Printed in Great Britain by Caligraving Ltd, Thetford

Contents

*The ordering of the collection within each section
is alphabetical by first line wherever possible.*

Introduction

The title of this collection of hymns, songs and chants is a phrase taken from one of my most popular songs, *The Tambourine Woman* (No. 109), and it was chosen to signify the link between earth and heaven – the spiritual and the material, and the inclusivity and faithfulness of God. It relates to many of the themes that colour my work, including the need for female figures within the Christian tradition, the role of music for community building, the cyclical nature of life and God's covenant within it, the importance of ecology and the interpenetration of the material world and the divine, the immanence of God in the Wisdom tradition, and the faithfulness of God's love. Inevitably, these have coloured and influenced my life as well, so that in trying to locate the wellsprings of my creativity in the context of my writing, they encompass both my sense of the spiritual in music, and the journey of feminist thought in the last quarter of the twentieth century.

My Theological Background

I was born at Lyndhurst in the New Forest in 1943, and raised in a culture of rural Anglicanism, from which I explored a number of alternative theological positions ranging from a fairly conservative evangelicalism to a fairly liberal Anglo-Catholicism. While working in London's Notting Hill after the race riots of 1960 I worshipped with Methodists for seven years – quite 'high' Methodists who tried a great deal of liturgical experiment and innovation. It was here that I encountered the 'protest' songs of Sydney Carter and the Christian Aid song contests organised by Brian Frost as *Songs from the Square*. I was also introduced to the publisher Bernard Braley, and through him became involved with the development of the Galliard imprint, which was at the forefront of the development of new liturgical material in this period. Here, above all, I learned about a God of challenge and a God of social justice, and these became two important themes in my work, for example in *Spirit of Justice* (No. 48) and *Who are these outside the barred gates* (No. 68).

For the last twenty-five years my main spiritual nurturing has been through a variety of 'alternative' liturgy groups, all embracing a strong feminist theology but by no means all composed exclusively of women. These groups were established as a result of the influx of feminist ideas and the associated dissatisfaction with the established churches, both Catholic and Protestant. Many pre-dated the ordination of women in the Anglican communion. Some met and continue meeting regularly, while others were more ad hoc in origin, brought together for particular events and occasions. Many felt sadly inadequate when it came to music in worship, an area where women need to feel re-empowered.

The Wimbledon Liturgy Group, now discontinued, involved both women and men. Music was often included, and we danced, wrote poems, shared meals and tried out ideas old and new. Womanchurch Reading is all women, and continues to meet regularly in the home of one of the group for worship and discussion. Liturgical experiment has become increasingly important to the group. There is usually a sharing of stories and poems on a particular theme, and then prayers together. We sometimes sing and dance, often using material from the anthology *Reflecting Praise* (Stainer & Bell/Women in Theology, 1993) and my song books. I wrote *Spring Song* (No. 76) for a spring liturgy and have tried out much material there, including my new one-person show entitled *Juggling – A Question of Identity*.

The London group of the Catholic Women's Network is all women, many of them Roman Catholic but some Anglican, who meet for a liturgical celebration followed by a shared meal. The elements of their worship are much like those of the Wimbledon group. The music varies from singing to or listening to tapes, to singing, either unaccompanied or with guitar or keyboard accompaniment. Sources are Iona songs, my songs, *Reflecting Praise,* Miriam Thérése Winter, the Taizé tradition and specially written songs. Circle dances are used regularly.

Key friends in this group for me are referred to throughout the book, but Ianthe Pratt needs special mention because of her Women's Resource Centre, the liturgies she regularly holds in her home, and the fact that she is often the one to whom I sing new hymns over the phone.

Three other contexts have been especially significant. One is Holy Rood House, the Centre for Health and Pastoral Care in Sowerby where I am a consultant for the Centre for Theology and Health, for which many of the hymns have been written. Elizabeth and Stanley Baxter have been important encouragers. Another is the Community of the Sisters of the Glorious Ascension in Prasada, Montauroux, where I stay on holiday with my friend, Pam Gladding. Many hymns have been written for services there. A third is the conference of the Hildegard Network that I founded in 1992 to explore the relationship of theology, healing and the arts.

No less important to me has been the discovery of the Wisdom traditions. A crucial guide on this journey was Julian of Norwich, whom I encountered at a crossroads in my life. Largely through the ministrations of the Beatles, Transcendental Meditation came to Britain in the 1960s, and I, like hundreds of others from many backgrounds, enthusiastically learnt its techniques. I had encountered nothing in church like the peace of my twenty-minute practice, and yet in Christian circles it was regarded with suspicion.

For me, the two were reconciled through the contemplative tradition, the way of unknowing and of darkness, which I found through Gonville ffrench-Beytagh, who had been Dean of Johannesburg but had been imprisoned and finally expelled because of his opposition to Apartheid. That for me was the beginning of the Wisdom journey. As with so much of my life, at first I did it my way. It was intimately connected with the feminine in God, and with finding the other half of one of the binary divides that characterise the Christian tradition: the darkness that balances the light; the unknowing that balances the aggressive pursuit of knowledge, which has led theology in patriarchal form to reduce God to a series of creedal statements; feminine images to balance male images; the accepting God to balance the judgemental God that peopled my childhood fears; and the intuitive God who cannot be held by the reasoning mind alone.

Through this experience and *The Creative Spirit*, my work on Hildegard of Bingen (Canterbury Press, 2000), I became essentially a Wisdom theologian. In Wisdom (whom I described as a blessed all-embracing darkness) I found a refuge from the worst excesses of the so-called Enlightenment which, though celebrated for its achievements, had forced an intellectual stranglehold on Europe since the late eighteenth century in a way much critiqued by feminist writers in many fields.

My Musical Background

My musical journey has shown a similar progression from strictness to freedom, and in the hymns and songs that have been written mostly in the last twenty-five years I have tried to gather together the insights gained from theology and musicology.

My grandfather had been a dance-band pianist in a New Forest village, and he played by ear; but he wanted his granddaughter to enter the world of classical music (epitomised by his 78rpm recording of José Iturbi paying Chopin's *Fantaisie-impromptu*). When he died I was too young to realise what I had missed by not learning his skills. In fact, as a child learning the piano I was glad of the containment of the classical tradition. I knew where I was by learning how to read the notes, and I enjoyed the poise and elegance of my favourite composers, Haydn and Mozart. A traditional training at Oxford University in the hidebound early 1960s reinforced these patterns of knowing through the study of history, analysis and written composition, activities steeped (as I later discovered) in a patriarchal, triumphalist tradition in which a single artist is identified with a work of art – whether that is a beautiful statue by Michelangelo or the lonely Handel creating the *Messiah* – mirroring a lonely God forming the world and separating himself from it.

In essence, my further musical journey represented an embracing of the musical freedom of different traditions and ways of music-making that were alien to this kind of classical training and attitudes as epitomised by an Oxford music degree. One step in this direction was made through the protest song movement in Notting Hill in the 1960s. I can recall a sense of rebellion in going back to Oxford to sing at my college and using a song entitled *O that Greedy Landlord*, which I accompanied on the guitar in an essentially classical programme. The scene was set for the embracing of musical diversity as a way of exploring different parts of my own psyche.

One route led me through contact with the English Folk Dance and Song Society, which freed up for me notions of 'correct' versions of tunes as opposed to those of a transformative, evolving tradition. Another route, soon after I left university, was through exploring sound with primary school children. New Age groups, ethnic traditions and music therapy have all proved absorbing to me. And whereas at first I was concerned about the diversity and discrepancies between the dominant classical tradition and the alternatives, now I rejoice in the diversity and realise that each represents a different aspect of my persona and can be respected in the same way that I taught respect for difference in the course in World Musics. This is as true internally as it is externally in terms of society.

All these currents came together for me in the mid 1980s, after a long period of chronic illness. I had begun to compose again, although Oxford had taught me that composers were usually male, German or French or Italian, and dead. I had discovered community music through playing folk guitar, and had dared to improvise in public. All these things were part of a process of healing and personal growth. Through the tradition of drumming, especially with my trusty djembe, I discovered an awareness of the role of my body in music-making that went much further than the classical concern with the effect of health on technical efficiency. Through explorations in Hinduism and New Age, I discovered people who genuinely believed in the transcendent power of music and, indeed, who could link this with the embodied art of dancing, in contrast to my puzzlement (as a deeply religious child) that choirs and congregations often had little sense of the religious meaning of what they sang.

Finally, in 1986, emerging from this difficult period and free at last from the anti-depressants I had been taking for some ten years, I started writing hymns. And the process of writing these early hymns – many of which were conceived on a lecture tour in Australia – was also a way of personal transformation.

The History of Women in Church Music

When I was seven, I was chosen to sing *O Jesus, I have promised* in the church hall at St Winifred's, Testwood, in the New Forest, but was not allowed to sing it in church, as only boys sang there. My puzzlement at this experience has, I believe, spurred me on in my lifelong quest to explore the history of women in liturgical music through the influence of feminist theologies. It is a history, until the second half of the last century, of the systematic exclusion of women both from the central mysteries of bread and wine and of music.

In spite of Christ's radical attitude to women, and ample evidence to suggest their equality with men in the early life and music of the church, in AD 325, when the emperor Constantine adopted Christianity as the official religion of the Roman Empire, an increasingly repressive orthodoxy replaced the diversity that had preceded it. Essentially, this involved a belief in the sinfulness of sex and the body, through which woman became a source of temptation, and through the associations with reproduction and childbirth, was given an inferior role to man.

Motherhood became degraded, in contrast to celibacy. The natural woman was condemned, and a form of chaste homosexual love was exalted. There was a systematic withdrawal of liturgical functions from women. Already in the Didascalia of AD 318 the singing of women in church was forbidden. In AD 367 the fourth canon of the Council of Laodicea stated that it was not fitting for women to draw near the altar nor to touch things which had been classed as the duty of men. In AD 379 the Synod of Antioch placed singing in the hands of professional men and boys. Funeral rites were transferred from the home to the church and in AD 392 the celebration of rituals in the home was discontinued. This curtailed women's liturgical authority at a stroke. Heretical sects like the Marianites, which included women scholars and liturgists, were persecuted mercilessly. Gnosticism became a heresy. Significantly, hymns for women to sing were now written by men, a pattern of putting words into women's mouths about such intimate functions as childbirth, marriage and death that continues to this day. As the body was considered sinful, dancing was banned, and the church extended its control to secular music.

It was through monasticism, paradoxically, and the separation of women from men in the religious orders, that some women's traditions were maintained through the singing of the seven Offices and the Eucharist. The tenth-century canoness Hroswitha knew Boethian music theory, and the twelfth-century abbess Herrad of Landsberg set poems to music and was an author and theologian. The best known of these remarkable figures, and for me a most powerful influence on my development as a composer, was Hildegard of Bingen (1098–1179), who wrote some seventy surviving compositions. In addition, her embracing of so many disciplines, including a variety of the arts, helped validate my own interdisciplinary approach to my work. I have translated her morality play with music, *Ordo Virtutum*, and over thirty of her songs. Some I have turned into metrical hymns, such as *Spirit of Fire* (No. 47, based on *O ignis spiritus)* and *Flourishing Branch* (No. 21, based on *O viridissima virga*). Especially at the Abtei St Hildegard in Germany I have felt her very close. I particularly remember working on her *Hymn to the Holy Spirit* and being faced with *O lorica vitae*. This could be rendered as 'breastplate', but I found that it also meant a woman's corset. Over my shoulder, I heard her 'yes' as I translated it as 'foundation garment of life'. In time I knew that she had taught me enough and I must go my own way. But I shall be eternally grateful for the role she played in my finding my identity both musically and theologically.

The development of polyphony, which required singers trained at university or choir school, excluded both women and amateur male musicians from composition and performance. It was only in the late Renaissance and then the Baroque periods that there was an upsurge of musical activity by women on both sides of the convent wall. Prominent in this revival were nuns who had received a musical education as part of their domestic upbringing. Italian convents were particularly renowned for their performance traditions. From the Middle Ages until the eighteenth century nuns were the only women who were relatively free to perform music publicly, involving instruments and in ensembles, and we have accounts of the excellence of these traditions from the sixteenth century. (This was later extended to girls and other women in the context of the remarkable Venetian ospedali.) In the convents, composing again flourished with nun composers like Isabella Leonarda (1620–1704). She was the last of the great nun polyphonic composers, as in the seventeenth century the tide of musical taste turned again and such activity was curtailed by a number of church injunctions, disobedience to which might involve excommunication.

The Reformation, meanwhile, had given an opportunity for change. In the nonconformist traditions, the sacred song allowed the mature woman's voice to be heard in worship. But Luther's establishment of the St Thomas School to provide boys for the choir showed how difficult it was to create a real difference. In England, boys' choir schools were established to serve the main churches and the cathedrals. Even now, though some English cathedrals have well-established girls' choirs, they lack the bequests that support the boys' choirs, and there are many who remain unhappy about any female presence. Because of the power of the past, the average church choir, short as it usually is of men, does not solve this problem by developing an alternative tradition of women, and this has developed freely only in some female religious communities, such as the Sisters of the Church, Ham Common, Richmond.

This brief historical outline shows clearly how, for much of its existence, the Christian Church has feared the participation of women. Although a few outstanding individuals such as Hildegard were tolerated or encouraged, a corporate women's tradition remained impossible until the late twentieth century, when the movement to put liturgical power into women's hands and the insights of feminist theologians coincided to create the possibility of change.

The Spirituality of Music

For much of the history of Western thought there has been an association perceived between music and spirituality, from the ancient goddess traditions and Plato through to Hildegard. But, in the hands of the thinkers and philosophers of the Enlightenment, the link between music and the spiritual became weakened. The search for the spiritual became an essentially human quest, located in the unconscious, and related to notions of self-fulfilment and self-actualisation.

However, for me, musical experience is about encounter; 'encounter with the Other' as Martin Buber described it in *I and Thou* (Charles Scribner's Sons, 1970). I have found it helpful to develop the metaphor of a variety of lenses or domains which interact as we compose, perform or listen to music, and which reflect the varied focus of the experiencer during the experience. The lenses are: expression – anOther self; values – anOther culture; construction – the world of abstract ideas; and materials – the environment.

All music draws its *Materials* from the body and the environment: every kind of vocal and instrumental tone colour, and sounds of nature and those of the acoustic space. Traditionally, the material of music has often been identified as the most humble element in the hierarchy of values. And yet it is possible with the most basic sounds and skills to enter the totality of the musical experience, if these areas are regarded as interlocking and not hierarchical. For example, produced with reverence and understanding, the complex sound of the Middle-Eastern Singing Bowl, rich in overtones, can have a powerful effect of calming and healing. Another example: a boy attended one of my workshops, and brought with him a Scottish pipe that he wished to play. For the workshop, he had learnt three notes, which he used to depict air in a piece performed in an ancient chapel, full of intense atmosphere and lit only with candles. In it he used his very limited and newly acquired technical skill to make unbelievably expressive sounds within the structure we had developed earlier. His father attended the performance and looked across at his son with an attitude of rapt attention that drew parent and child together timelessly. It was a deeply spiritual and personal experience that involved all the domains, but which was entered with limited expertise in the area of materials.

In the area of *Expression*, concerned with the evocation of mood and individual or corporate emotion, and with images, memories and atmosphere on the part of all those involved in the musical performance, there is a powerful intersection of the subjectivity of composer, performer and listener. Listeners may bring extrinsic meaning to the music – meaning that has been locked on to that particular piece, style or tradition through personal associations. Popular music, in particular, often involves such identifications, as in the phrase 'They're playing our tune'.

This experience of encounter in the expressive domain may be through the music itself or another person within the musical experience, as this is an area of empathy, imagination and creation of identity. Singing songs from different cultures can, for example, give children a chance to empathise with the unknown 'other'. Asked to sing a black township prayer in my cantata *The Healing of the Earth*, one child said

'When I sing that song to myself I think that somehow I am part of those people you talked about so far away.'

Appropriate degrees of repetition and contrast are important in defining *Construction*. How contrast is handled within a tradition – the degree to which it is tolerated – partly defines the idiom and may be regulated by the tradition's elders, be they the Beckmessers of Western classical music or the master drummers of Yoruba. In pop music, repetition can be more overt and acceptable than in art traditions, except where repetition is stylised and attracts a broader, 'crossover' audience as is with minimalism. Analysis and teaching of the Western canon has focused on this area. It is here, too, that many claims have been made by aestheticians for a spiritual association with order, linked with such ideas as the music of the spheres.

Value relates to the context of the musical experience, and links it with culture and society. All musical experiences are culturally related and must be recontext-ualised in a different culture. The individual constructivist model of education has often ignored this. The musical experience contains both implicit (within the music) and explicit (within the context) value systems. However, these two areas of value interact powerfully. Notions of internal values are a subject of debate in musicological circles, but as soon as a text is present – either in the music or associated with it – value systems will be declared, as in the hymn and song traditions. As music and society are inextricably linked, so too are church and culture. Their values lie at the heart of our religious traditions and our worship music, whether instrumental or vocal, 'abstract' or functional.

The model of these domains enables us to examine a musical experience through four lenses and to see the focus of the experiencer and intersection of the domains at any given point in the process as central. Through the domains we can measure the effectiveness of the musical experience and analyse it – discover, for example, how music developed in the context of small gatherings of women, concerned to develop feminist approaches to Christian ritual.

Whereas these four domains exist as overlapping circles in the experience, spirituality can be found, I suggest, in the relationship between these areas. I define it as the ability to transport the audience to a different time–space dimension, to move it from everyday reality to 'another world'. Subsumed within my own thinking and related to spirituality are a number of ideas, including flow, ecstasy, trance, mysticism, peak experiences, the religious experience and liminality, a concept developed by the theatre anthropologist Victor Turner, who draws on an analysis of ritual.

The notion of transformation is central to religious ritual, be it the Christian Eucharist or a shamanic healing rite, and can encompass both the personal and communal. There are parallel stages in any ritual: 'severance, transition and return'. Severance is associated with leaving everyday life by means of ritual gestures such as holding hands or lighting candles. In the transitional or liminal phase there is contact with the transpersonal, which may take the form of change of consciousness. The return phase signals a coming back to earth and the beginning of a new life. It is possible to identify these moments in a musical piece even when not associated with ritual, and to relate accounts of transformation through experiencing music with this concept.

The spiritual experience is defined as an apprehension of a perfect fit between all the domains. As the following account shows, this may happen gradually:

> For the first twenty-five minutes I was totally unaware of any subtlety ... whilst wondering what, if anything, was supposed to happen during the recital.
>
> What did happen was magic! After some time, insidiously the music began to reach me. Little by little, my mind – all my senses it seemed – were becoming transfixed. Once held by these soft but powerful sounds, I was irresistibly drawn into a new world of musical shapes and colours. It almost felt as if the musicians were playing me rather than their instruments, and soon, I, too, was clapping and gasping with everyone else ... I was unaware of time, unaware of anything other than the music. Then it was over. But it was, I am sure, the beginning of a profound admiration that I shall always have for an art form that has been until recently totally alien to me.
>
> Ian Dunmore: Sitar Magic, *Nadaposana One*
> (London: Editions Poetry, 1983, pp.20–21)
> *[Copyright holder untraced]*

In this testimony, the materials of the sound and the 'shapes' of the construction were gradually integrated within the experiencer's being to become fused with the experience, as represented symbolically in the following diagram.

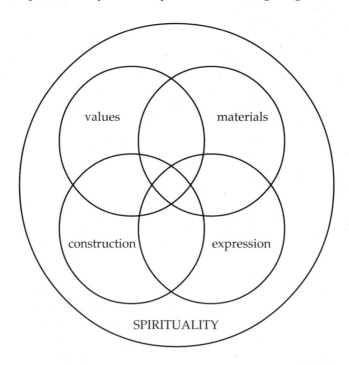

Figure 1: The complete spiritual experience

Conversely, there is no spiritual experience where dissatisfaction is present in one area, or conflict exists between several areas.

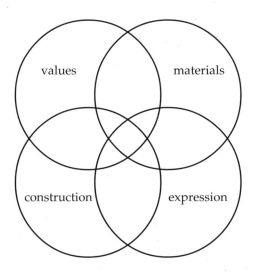

Figure 2: A musical experience with no spiritual domain

The area of the effectiveness of values is at least partly dependent on the context, which will set up various associational processes resonating through all the domains of the experience. Further reflective processes will make these links stronger so that a certain set of associational patterns become linked with that piece or its style. Once, in Greece, I encountered a group of orthodox worshippers who were deeply racist and homophobic. Turning on the television that Sunday morning to hear Greek orthodox chanting, formerly for me an uplifting experience, I now found my satisfaction clouded by their value system. In this story we encounter the distinction between reflected-upon and unreflected-upon experience, and the role of meta-awareness.

On the other hand, values may also be reinforced by associations, as in the case of a feminist's relationship to pieces by women. If these relational associations are benign to the experiencer then the level of absorption will be increased. It explains why feminists have real problems with so much religious music, with its non-inclusive language and its triumphal or exclusivist themes and its failure to express effectively the vulnerability of God.

I reached an important stage on my own musical and theological journey when, inspired by the insights of feminist theology and groups such as Women in Theology, I started to write pieces that embodied alternative value systems. No longer sharing the values of traditional hymnody in such areas as inclusive language, substitution theologies of redemption, and the omnipotence and separateness of God from creation, I nonetheless understood that it is by hymns, far more than sermons and even prayers, that the theology of the church is transmitted. Words and music in combination leave deep impressions on the memory. I saw the urgent need for new hymns to reflect the ideas of the feminist theologians. I started with the Celtic tradition that provided a valuable link with the past for feminist theology, and I versified a number of texts, such as *Give thou to me, O God* (No. 85), which has become popular for healing services.

Through feminist theology closely associated with ecotheology, I was also inspired by the reassertion of subjugated value systems. In the following diagram of the relative polarities, items on the right are those that are dominant in Western culture. Those on the left, in contrast, are the ones most often reasserted by feminist theologians, and are among the qualities I have attempted to reflect in my hymns, songs and chants.

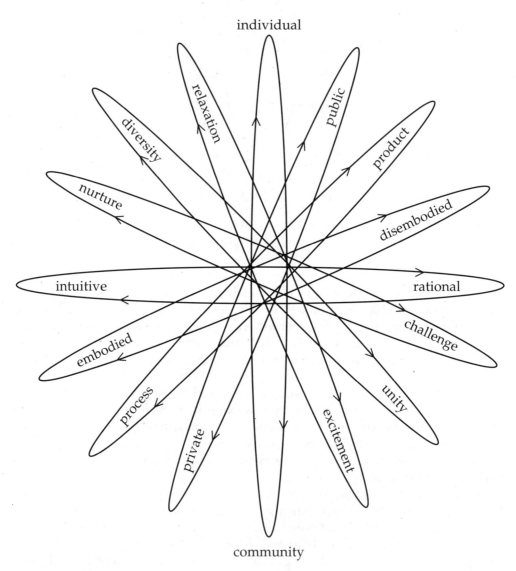

Figure 3: Value systems

Individual – Community

Even within the church, with its stress on 'my salvation', our society is individualistic, yet the community of the Gospels is one of inclusion. Moreover, music has always played a significant role in building the community of the church. Inclusion has always been part of the feminist agenda, and the absence of this theme from traditional hymns led me to an inclusive position in my early song *The Tambourine*

Woman (No. 109), and in my hymn *We shall go out with hope of resurrection* (No. 63), with its closing line: 'Including all within the circles of our love.'

The Tambourine Woman also relates to the natural world and the theme of ecotheology, in which I have been influenced by the ecotheologian Mary Grey, especially *Redeeming the Dream: Feminism, Redemption and Christian Tradition* (SPCK, 1989). In hymns such as *Deep inside creation's mystery* (No. 15), rocks, stones, insects and birds join human beings in the cosmic song, and in *Come, sparkling water* (No. 80) the elements are used to indicate 'sacred endings and beginnings'. For me the theme reached its culmination in *Song of the Earth*, which sees us as part of the great song on which all parts of the planet contribute, and which is included in my cantata for children for the Queen's Golden Jubilee, *The Healing of the Earth*.

Another issue central to the feminist agenda, also reflected in my hymn texts, is that of inclusive language. The story is ongoing, for there still remains some resistance within the church to its use. For the hymn writer, two interesting challenges are involved. The first is technical: to find non-male descriptions for people and (more significant in the hymn traditions) the use of the word human and not the word 'man' as a generic term for human beings. Of course, one avoids gender-defining pronouns in the third person singular – the plural presents fewer problems – but words like 'brothers' need to be used with 'sisters', which may have a knock-on effect within the constraints of metre. Adaptations of past hymns tend to encounter resistance, and I have found it more effective to rewrite the ideas of an existing text completely rather than change the odd word. So, *Let all the stars in heaven* (No. 34) was for me a reclaiming of Sydney Carter's *Every star shall sing a carol*.

The second problem-area is poetical and theological: the need for a 'feminine divine', or at least an inclusive-gender God to extend inclusive language to the divine. In the Marian tradition, Mary is close to this condition, and I began with two examples in the genre of Marian hymnody: *Mary, our mother* (No. 36) and *Mary, chosen to be mother* (No. 37). In *God the Artist* (No. 93) and *Birth Song* (No. 90) I also used the first person singular for God. The truly inclusive solution, which I have used for much of my work, is to use non-gendered words such as friend, companion, and healer, as in an early hymn about inclusive language, *Count Me In* (No. 42).

However, there is in addition a need for specifically feminine images for God to balance the 2000-year-old tradition of male names. Janet Wootton's hymn *Dear Mother God* is a fine example of how this can be done. It was only quite late in my writing journey that I could bring myself to create hymns using a feminine divine. I first used the pronoun 'she' for the Holy Spirit in *It was dark in the dawn of time* (No. 31). And in my *Hymn for 100 Years of Women's Ordination* (No. 60), composed for the centenary celebrations of the first woman priest in the United Kingdom, I used feminine images to access the wrath of God at the treatment of women by the church.

Unity – Diversity

The Christian Church in Europe has put a high premium on unity, and on the dominance of a single metanarrative to link its monotheism with a concern for the privileging of order over chaos. Correspondingly, chaos is demonised, as in Marriott and Raffles' famous lines: 'Thou whose almighty word / Chaos and darkness heard,/ And took their flight'.

Feminist theology has problematised such thinking, and it was the darkness that interested me in the first hymn I wrote, *There is darkness in the night-time* (No. 54). It has continued to do so, as in the much later text *It was dark in the dawn of time* (No. 31). This has not been without problems for others, as in the line 'God of order, God of chaos', in the hymn *God of justice, wind the circle* (No. 24), commissioned for the millennium celebrations by Churches Together in Britain and Ireland.

In addition, contrasting with the dominant concept of the permanence of God, feminism has embraced the notion, which dates back to the Greek pre-Socratic philosopher Heraclitus, that reality is continually in flux, like the cycle of change in women's bodies. I embraced this in the song *Life Cycle* (No. 75). More recently, in my song *A-godding* (No. 74), I have experimented with the ideas of process theology, moving towards God-as-Verb. The self is seen as mobile and changing, as in the song *Been there, done that* (No. 92); and, in several texts, I have borrowed from the carnival tradition the possibility of a multiplicity of identities, giving greater freedoms for the self. 'You mean I can be many things?' is a comment expressed with great joy in my workshops. Women by nature may be more aware than men of juggling multiple identities. Is the mother hunting for a child's lost trainer really the same person as the self-assured teacher standing in front of a class?

When the personality seems to be in pieces, there is also a link with the experience of suffering. The philosopher Gillian Rose has developed the notion of 'the broken middle', the necessity for living with the contradictions, also linked by Mary Grey with religious ideas of the underworld. In dealing with the story of Psyche and Eros, Mary Grey sees reflected in the myth the problems Western society has when facing real-life death and dying – issues I have tried to address in *Grief* (No. 17).

With these debates to re-evaluate diversity has come the possibility of using insights and materials from other faiths. This was the policy Janet Wootton and I adopted as editors of the anthology *Reflecting Praise*, in which we included the beautiful Hindu hymn *My mother you are and my father you are*.

I have also experimented with multilinguality in a single song in *Weaving Wisdom's Circle* (No. 165), where each section of the round is in a different language: French, German and English, the official languages of the Women's Synod in Gmunden, Austria. One participant reported that the way the different languages fitted together made it, for her, the sound of heaven.

Public – Private

This domain, with its distinction between male-public and female-domestic-private, has always been central in determining the position of women in Western society. And the quest of marginalised groups to use alternative spaces, as well as to move from the private to the public arena, has been the source of much that is creative in the movement of feminist theology since the 1970s, when books like Susie Orbach's *Fat is a Feminist Issue* demonstrated powerful linkages between women's intimate, often very carefully hidden, struggles and the wider society. The slogan of feminists in the 1970s was that 'the personal is political', and this became a powerful rallying cry linking the private struggles of many women with wider socio-political issues.

Such groups have proved important staging posts between the public and private, and their existence has been alternately accepted and rejected by the mainstream church as they have waxed or waned in strength of voice, and raised unresolved issues concerning sexuality, language and ritual.

They have also provided an important context for women's music-making, and much of my material was first created for and sung by them. They have provided significant testing grounds for new musical ideas and ways of knowing and working, and a crucible for experimentation with more public worship. While I have in part felt myself following a well-established route, pioneered by hymn writers such as Cecil Frances Alexander and Fanny Crosby, I have also tried to foster material for public situations from which women have traditionally been excluded; with the 'Magnificat Project' (1999–2006) for example, commissioning six women to compose settings of the Magnificat and Nunc Dimittis with funds from Women in Theology and Women in Music.

Inevitably, debates in the area of feminist theology centre on the public authority of women and on their ordination, and many of my hymns were written as presents for the first generation of women priests – hymns such as *Praise to you, our great Creator* (No. 44) and *Called to serve in our uniqueness* (No. 9). Another, *We shall go out with hope of resurrection* (No. 63) was written for a liturgy asking for women priests organised by Nicola Slee in Southwark Cathedral in 1992, and I am proud of the fact that it has acquired the status of a minor anthem associated with women's ordination in Anglicanism.

I have also written many hymns and songs for Catholic Women's Ordination, for example *The Vision* (No. 89), composed for the women's pilgrimage before the Ottowa conference of Women's Ordination Worldwide in July 2005. An especially happy occurrence, in Seneca Falls, was when the great granddaughter of Elizabeth Cady Stanton heard our singing and said that, still fighting on for women's rights we were in the tradition of her ancestor. The gathering in Dublin in 2000 of Women's Ordination Worldwide was a huge example of 'going public', and it provoked confrontation with the religious authorities. Austrian women have been irregularly ordained in central Europe for some time, and I assisted with the music for the ordinations on the St Lawrence River at Gananoque in Canada in 2005, where I joyfully sang Hildegard's *Antiphon to Wisdom*. On 10 April 2003 Elizabeth Stuart was consecrated as Bishop in the Province for Open Episcopal Ministry and Jurisdiction in the United Kingdom, and for her I wrote *Wisdom Song* (No. 96), emphasising her vocation and the challenging nature of the Wisdom tradition.

In hymns like *Within our hearts may truth arise* (No. 69) I have tried to assimilate the ideas of theologians such as Myra Poole and Dorothee Soelle, in particular *The Silent Cry: Mysticism and Resistance* (Augsburg Fortress, 2001), making connections between private prayer and public action. Other hymns give voices to women whose stories had not so far been told, as in *Mary, Mary, let down your hair* (No. 104), participating in a tradition originating with early hymn writers such as the Greek Orthodox nun Cassia. In the *Gospel of Mary*, which formed part of the Nag Hammadi library, I found that the struggle for women's authority started as a dispute among the disciples between Mary Magdalene and Peter. Her authority was based on her reception of the first resurrection appearance, whereas Peter's was based on the words of Jesus: 'On this rock I will found my Church.' Peter won, but the struggle is still around.

Whatever the consequences of the debate about women's authority and priestly and musical leadership, there seem to be certain practical consequences when women are present and active in liturgical gatherings. Often, the model is one of shared authority, with, for example, consecration of the elements by the group, though avoiding symbols of bread and wine in favour of hazelnuts, apples or honey. Similarly, there can be an emphasis on the amateur as opposed to the professional, and the 'community chorus' as opposed to the solo voice.

To answer the needs of these new conditions, a repertoire of material has grown over the last three decades. One of the first collections to answer the challenge was *Women Included* (SPCK, 1991), which grew out of the work of the St Hilda Community in London. *Reflecting Praise* is a hymn book celebrating the work of women past and present, as well as men who use 'softer' images for God, and it was the first collection to concentrate on women's contribution to hymnody with both words and music. *Human Rites: Worship Resources for an Age of Change*, edited by Hannah Ward and Jennifer Wild (Mowbray/Continuum, 1995), is a collection of liturgies from alternative worshipping groups, an anthology not of pre-set liturgies imposed by some 'official' committee or commission, but of what ordinary people are doing in their worship.

Product – Process

Oracy, the spoken word as the prime means of communication, is increasingly marginalised in our society, where literacy reinforces our product-based Western culture and values. Theologically, this has contributed to the canonisation of the text, and with it a general stifling of debate.

Two occurrences in my own life brought home this fact to me. In the 1950s my mother was warned that I asked too many questions in my confirmation class. I was given the catechism to learn and accept; there was neither argument nor compromise, and the end of any discussion was carefully contrived to produce that acceptance. Later, as an undergraduate, I experienced something similar with the Christian Union. Given the InterVarsity Declaration of Faith, I was asked to assent to all its statements. After a night of study, thought and prayer, I decided that I could assent to all but two of them. But they told me it was all or nothing, and so I never joined. Faith in these contexts is reduced to the status of an assent to a series of doctrinal statements, usually arising from a privileged reading of the canonical texts, to be consumed like a pre-packaged meal for one's own good, and with merely illusory 'discussion' intended to make for more palatable consumption.

With the canonisation of texts and music into a 'museum' of decontextualised liturgy there is an accompanying emphasis on the excellence of the product – the singing of the liturgy by our fine cathedral choirs, for example – to enshrine its message in the unchanging permanence of art. However, within the contemporary movement of women's liturgy there has been a contrary emphasis on oracy and improvisation as a route to flexibility, openness and innovation. Sometimes, the circumstances in which it arises are as if oracy had never been challenged. In several convents I have found that there is no systematic scoring of material, and there is little desire to retain or to preserve it. Repertoire is freely changed and learnt orally. Printed handouts, if any, are to be retained only as necessary, perhaps for reworking to fit changing contexts. The same is often true for small liturgy groups.

In contrast, in a workshop where groups of women were asked to create liturgies from aspects of the Easter story, those who encountered the greatest difficulty were those who started from printed resources. Far from stimulating their creativity, it appeared to stifle their talent to rework from their own memories, and to experience symbolic actions, words and songs appropriate to the context. People who prefer oracy to literacy in our culture (and in general women are more skilled than men in oral discourse) reflect this capacity to remember material in ways appropriate to any situation in which they find themselves. In effect, to improvise.

In my own work I have tried to revalue the ephemeral over the fixed process, and to restore the liberating spirit of improvisation. In *Life Cycle* (No. 75) and *The hope goes round* (No. 51) I have also tried to express something of the cyclical nature of women's experience, rooted in her bodily processes and fitting uneasily with male constructs of the world as product-based work. Within improvisation, any outcome is regarded simply as a moment in an ongoing process, and the repeated chord sequences of many of my chants such as *Come, Holy Spirit* (No. 136) lend themselves to improvised singing, just as the round, which I have also used, favours process over finite, completed musical statement.

Absence of definitive story forms, fluidity in structures that are freely flowing rather than linear and analytical, an increased subjectivity, and transmission through the spoken rather than written word are all characteristics of orate cultures that are also shared with women's liturgies. They foster an open religion rather than one based on unchanging, book-based revelation. And with them come a scope for happy accidents and humour that is alien to the fixed, written down tradition. Among The Holy Fools, a group of people who clown and improvise in religious contexts, I have witnessed remarkable insights arising on the spur of the moment in a way quite impossible had events been planned (see Nos. 104 and 111).

Excitement – Relaxation

Western society feeds on stimulation and excitement. To value the slower rhythms of the natural or agrarian world, or above all to treasure stillness and silence, is to be boring, not 'cool' – almost a crime.

But running contrary to this frenetic mode, there has been an increasing focus on meditation as an alternative to contemporary lifestyles, and reclaiming time for silence and reflection has formed an important part of women's liturgies. Inevitably, this has brought the movement into conflicting positions with established religious thought and practice.

In liturgical music, the thirst for excitement has often been reflected in the triumphalism of many hymns – *Onward, Christian soldiers* is a perfect case in point, both in its words and music. Moreover, the patriarchal church still presents us with a plethora of sounds and images strikingly projected, with the intention of their message being instantly absorbed, without space for contemplation, or the chance to relate it to everyday experience. And the medium for these images has been literate, whether verbal or musical, not oral and improvised, so their expression has been canonic and inflexible.

Of course it is possible to use sound recordings of rivers or waterfalls as an aid to contemplation, but the idea of a 'sacred space' they foster is artificial, not grounded in everyday reality. To create their own music, to engage with a slower tempo through music in the real world has been a fascinating challenge for feminist musicians, as they have rediscovered both a variety of meditative traditions, and the role of music to function as a raft for reflection and healing by the absorption of ideas, sounds and images presented to and from the depth of one's being.

Symbolic of the challenge to find new sounds for worship has been the organ, whose aural and architectural presence dominates most churches. Although capable of gentle sounds, it is characterised by many women as loud and dominant, and it is usually played by men. Where groups of worshipping women do have access to large liturgical spaces that include an organ, there is often a resistance to its use as a musical representation of a triumphalist and overbearing theology.

In contrast, the preferred instruments for informal private groups have been guitars and flutes, and more exotic additions such as the singing bowl. The drum may also feature in feminist worship. I have always favoured it in my own music-making, but because of its connections with male musicians and militarism, many women find it hard to make any identification. When appropriated from other cultures such as Native American and African, it is also the case that their drumming traditions are those of men, women being restricted to rattles or instruments like tambourines. Interestingly, in workshops women tell of how at school they wanted to play the drums, but were never allowed to because the boys shouted louder and the teachers wanted to keep them quiet! So there is a good case for reclaiming the instrument, which in essence is simply an energiser of a neutral power that can be used for destructive or constructive purposes – for example, to empower action for social justice.

Within the search for a new balance, it is also possible to revisit 'strong' tunes and texts. While I have written a number of Taizé chants, I have also reworked *Thine be the glory* to include the chorus 'We can share your darkness; we can share your life'. When I used the stronger tune for *To God be the glory* for the *Hymn for 100 Years of Women's Ordination* (No. 60) I was told that women would dislike it because it was too forceful. But by then I had rediscovered some of the spirit of the suffragettes, who had not been afraid of powerful melodies. The hymn recalls a renowned fighter for women, Gertrude von Petzold, and when it was first sung at the Britain and Ireland School of Feminist Theology at Bristol University in 2004, women got their scarves out and waved them like a football crowd. I felt I had got it right!

Challenge – Nurture

The pursuit of excitement and the dominant myth of the heroic journey have led to a profoundly challenging society that devalues nurture and counts violence and death above birth and growth. Added to this, there is a strong sense that the dominant patriarchal traditions have been very hard for women, whether in their relationship to original sin and to their own bodies, or in the stress on the maleness of God and on the glorification of human suffering. If the dominant signifier is ultimately the phallus, then the judgemental God of the *Dies Irae* or of Cardinal Newman's eschatological poem *The Dream of Gerontius* makes women's position fragile, fragmented and ambiguous.

In contrast, many feminists would prefer a theology based on Julian's vision that 'All shall be well, all shall be well and all manner of thing shall be well,' an aspiration that inspired my hymn *All shall be well, in love enclosed* (No. 6). In addition, while attention has been drawn to the loss of female generativity in European symbolism, the need for nurturing underpins much of the theology of women's spirituality groups, so that metaphors of female nurturing now feature strongly in hymns and songs, and are used with confidence to balance the male images predominating for the last 2000 years.

These ideas have started a radical shift in Christology. Rather than being a male saviour, Jesus can become a model of human flourishing, an insightful teacher, and a person of humour and compassion. In concentrating on the themes of birth and nourishing, we are returning to the very roots of Christian theology.

Rational – Intuitive

The Enlightenment was based on the Cartesian rallying cry of 'Cogito, ergo sum', and modern Western culture continues to value reason above intuition. Under its influence, the intuitive aspects of the Christian religion were suppressed in favour of theological codifications, and the ideal of objectivity played a crucial part in tyrannising groups of all kinds by means of notions of normality. The story, the oldest route of transmission for wisdom between generations, was devalued in favour of the book and the lecture, and, in methodological terms, stories were reduced to the 'merely anecdotal'.

Most feminist theologians, on the other hand, have based their theologies on personal experience. The centrality of lived experience to feminist theology reflects the role of Wisdom in the Hebrew Bible. In broadening the scope of this exploration, the role of the visionary experience has likewise been rediscovered and re-evaluated, with a wave of interest in medieval female mystics like Julian of Norwich, Margery Kempe and Hildegard of Bingen.

As one who regularly presents these women dramatically, I find it notable that, following performances, women in particular will seek validation of their own visionary experiences. Sometimes they might start tentatively, with statements like 'I have never shared this with anyone before but ...' The telling of the stories of women of the past as a way of validating the experience of contemporary women has helped to redress the oppression of their intuitive responses. And from an encounter with New-Age spiritualities even a term such as 'angel' may be re-assessed, not as a superstition from a bygone and irrational past, but as a metaphor that finds expression in women's groups, and in songs such as *We light the candles here* (No. 127) and, in a lighter vein, *Angel in my Soul* (No. 115).

Embodied – Disembodied

With its roots in Christianity, Western society has retained the dichotomy of body and soul, and added another 'detachable' element: the mind or intellect. To reconcile the split between ideas and action, the praxis model of theology is much favoured amongst feminist theorists, and I have attempted to reflect their insights in my words and music. The activism of feminist theologians is seen in their involvement in movements such as the ordination of women, reproductive rights, the struggle against global capitalism and against sexual violence, and their work for environmental justice. For example, Mary Grey has moved beyond the classical dualisms to see a God immanently and intimately involved in struggles for communal and individual justice in what she calls 'epiphaneous action'.

Many of my songs are about social justice, which has become a dominant theme in my work, as in a hymn written for a visit of the controversial gay Episcopalian Bishop Gene Robinson to Britain in 2005, *God of empowerment, spiralling Wisdom* (No. 23), with its challenging statements about the concern of Jesus for the marginalised. This concentration on the vulnerability of God and God's immanence in human suffering is a recurring theme in feminist theology and liturgy.

I have also used bodily images and have written circle dances such as *Peace flowing outward and peace flowing in* (No. 43). All my performances end with circle dances. One in particular, which included people with movement difficulties, was deeply moving. Here, in a circle dance, all the less-able-bodied were supported in the circle by one another and the able-bodied, and the power of the circle became very telling.

*   *   *   *   *

We live in interesting times when, uniquely, there are both new ways of seeing the feminine in God, and a growing number of women in positions of authority – at least in the Protestant and Nonconformist churches. The achievement of women working in small liturgy groups has been to create a fresh and original corpus of material and to change attitudes. There remains a great deal to be done before the accepted public and corporate voice of the church ceases to be that of men, and before the model of the body of Christ ceases to be male. But the systematic exclusion of women from the mainstream of Christian music-making is over. Hidden traditions have been recovered. The moral claims of inclusive language are increasingly accepted, and even the enshrined culture of our church and collegiate choirs has not proved impregnable to the presence of women.

It is in this context that my work is set, reflecting its themes and aspirations. This collection affirms some of the ways of knowing that have been marginalised by Western society, and it affirms the need for the valuing of connection, intuition, process, holistic healing, and collaboration, passion and commitment. Like many women before me, I have tried to reflect in song the visionary, improvisatory, integrative, authoritative nature of God. I hope that *A Rainbow to Heaven* will encourage other women to do the same, and to have the courage to sing, play, compose and improvise. For music is power.

June Boyce-Tillman
May 2006

Acknowledgements

The names of many who have helped me on my journey are to be found in this book, and I am deeply grateful to them all. In this sense, the corpus of my work is also a 'collaborative' achievement. Others I wish to thank are those who have supported me through my most difficult days and kept faith in my creativity:

The Benedictine Community at the Abtei St Hildegard, Eibingen, Germany
Sister Aileen CSC and the Community of the Sisters of the Church at Ham Common, Richmond, Surrey
The Rev. Canon Ian Ainsworth-Smith
The Revs. Elizabeth and Stanley Baxter and the community at Holy Rood House
The community at Bickersteth House
The late Bernard Braley
Dr Carolyn Boulter
Catholic Women's Network/Women, Word, Spirit
Cecile and Jean CGA at Prasada, Montauroux, France
Professor Chris and Isabel Clarke
The Rev. Doug Constable
The Rev. Charles and Chris Dodd
Penelope Eckersley
The community of the Episcopal Divinity School, Cambridge, Massachusetts, USA
Professor Michael Finnissy
The late Rev. Canon Gonville ffrench-Beytagh
Pam Gladding
Professor Mary Grey
Professor Grenville Hancox
Dr Graham Harvey
The Hildegard Network
Professor Lisa Isherwood
The late Professor Mike Llewellyn
The Community of the Sisters of the Love of God, The convent of the incarnation, Fairacres, Oxford
Mary Jo and Patrice SSHM at the Noddfa Retreat Centre at Penmaenmawr
The late Sister Mary Paul OB and the Benedictine Community at St Mary's Abbey, West Malling
The Rev. Jean Mayland
The Rev. David Page
Myra Poole CND
Ianthe Pratt

continued overleaf

Dr Ian Sharp
The St Julian's Community
The Rt Rev. Professor Elizabeth Stuart
My sons, Matthew and Richard Tillman
The Rev. Canon Andrew Todd
The University of Winchester
The Rev. Dr Janet Wootton

Hymns

My hymns follow the linear and theological patterns of the Protestant hymn, incorporating feminist theologies into their structures, especially in the area of using women's experience. They are in established metres, and are easily assimilated into church liturgies. Much is possible within the restraints of a metrical form, which can be both an inspiration and a link with tradition. Where well-known tunes are used, the old text will also resonate in the minds of those singing. Regarding rhyme I am more cautious, and remain doubtful about the manipulations it may require of the language. There were few rhymes in my early attempts at versifying Celtic texts, and I sense that in a hymn such as *We shall go out with hope of resurrection* an absence of rhyme may be a strength.

Although my hymns in general have four-part harmony, many were first sung as single melodies. They may still be performed in this way, with the tune pitched to suit the mood and age of the group. When people are tired or have colds, they need lower material than when they are lively and excited – fixed pitched instruments have not helped us to make our material more accessible. For me, the unaccompanied human voice is the most flexible of instruments, and I delight in finding the appropriate register for any place and occasion intuitively, with a note plucked from the air. This is the contextualisation of music, and it resembles the contextualisation of biblical texts asked for by the feminist theologians.

Where the hymns contain personal narratives, these are explained in the accompanying note. Many of these texts reflect the presence of two places that have fired my creativity: Holy Rood House, with its challenge to create effective new liturgy; and Prasada, in the depths of Provence, with its stimulus to create material for the more unusual feasts. Another important influence has been the creative liturgies of the Catholic Women's Network.

I am a musician, and I endeavour to make the meaning of the words fit the contours of the melody. For most of the hymns I have at some point written my own tune. This is particularly challenging when I have worked hard at the marriage of text and tune with the original, but on occasion it can also enable me to provide an illuminating harmony to highlight the theology. I regard this fusion in the light of Hildegard's statement in *Scivias* 3.13.1 that the words represent the body and humanity while the melody represents the soul and divinity, so that the perfect matching of words and melody in a beautiful hymn brings body, soul, humanity and divinity into unity.

1 Father's Day

1 A father stoops to lift a weary toddler;
   His warming hug will drive away the fear;
   He can fulfil the needs of growing children;
   When danger threatens, he is standing near.

2 The child grows up and flexes youthful muscles;
   The body fills out to maturity;
   The father watches firmly on the sidelines,
   Delighting in such creativity.

3 For he has learned the arts of human parents
   From God's creating deep at work inside,
   Where gentle pity comforts human weakness
   And hands of love lie strong and open wide.

4 May all who choose a way as human parents
   Rest in those strengthening hands that can uphold,
   Draw loving from the source of all creation;
   So when that path is rough, they will stay bold.

This text, to be sung to INTERCESSOR, was written at the Abtei St Hildegard in August 1993, in response to a request made at the Hymn Society conference for a hymn for Father's Day.

Metre: 11.10.11.10.

2   St Bartholomew

ST BARTHOLOMEW

Traditional North American
arranged June Boyce-Tillman (1943–)

A fig tree is lean - ing its branch - es down low__ To pro- -tect a young man__ from the sun's mid-day glow, In__ deep me - di - ta - tion, he's find - ing his way, Through the vi - sion that Ja - cob re-ceived as he prayed. Al - le- -lu - ia to Je - sus who died on a tree__ And has raised up a lad - der of sal- -va - tion for me, And has raised up a lad - der of sal - va - tion for me.

Arrangement © Copyright 2006 Stainer & Bell Ltd

For Jean, Cecile and Pam

1 A fig tree is leaning its branches down low
 To protect a young man from the sun's midday glow,
 In deep meditation, he's finding his way,
 Through the vision that Jacob received as he prayed.
 Alleluia to Jesus who died on a tree
 And has raised up a ladder of salvation for me,
 And has raised up a ladder of salvation for me.

2 His neighbour is calling, 'I've found a good friend.'
 He hears the new story, brings his prayer to an end.
 He is doubtful, but trusts as he follows his heart
 To a curious teacher who may Wisdom impart.
 Chorus

3 Jesus welcomes him, saying: 'I have known you before,
 I have seen your integrity, based on ancient lore.
 Things greater than these you will see with your eyes.'
 'Such truth comes from God,' is the man's quick reply.
 Chorus

4 May we follow truth as Bartholomew of old;
 Meditation and prayer in our lives will unfold
 Deep Wisdom that calls us to help people see
 The route to the mystery that sets us all free.
 Chorus

My good friend Pam Gladding has shared many wonderful holidays with me and a great deal of my creativity. When we stay at Prasada with Jean and Cecile CGA our visits coincide with the festival of St Bartholomew, the patron saint of the village. This is an amazing event bringing together the Christian and the pre-Christian (pagan) very effectively. The effigy of the Duc d'Epernon is burned one night with associated jubilation and dancing. On the festival day the relics of St Bartholomew are solemnly processed through the village with the pipes and drums of the Provençal dancing traditions and a sprig of vine. These sometimes play for the procession in the church when they yield to the organ for the rest of the worship. The service is followed by folk dancing and aperitifs in the square. It is a wonderfully syncretic mix that can teach us a great deal about the peaceful co-existence of various traditions. The story of the call of Bartholomew–Nathaniel recalls the story of Jacob's ladder. This is the reason for the use of a tune from a song associated with that story – from which the words of the chorus are also taken.

3 Friendship

ALEXINA SM

June Boyce-Tillman (1943–)

A mo-ther with her child Be-side a fo-reign stream, A-
-fraid of an-cient E-gypt's might Pre-serves her lov-ing dream.

* The guitar chords will not fit with the choral harmonies.

1 A mother with her child
 Beside a foreign stream,
 Afraid of ancient Egypt's might
 Preserves her loving dream.

2 Come, weave the rushes tight
 And fill the cracks with tar;
 The tide will be your messenger
 And bear your baby far.

3 Let us weave baskets now
 From welcome hands of friends;
 For these will bear us safely on
 Towards our journey's end.

4 Between these linking arms
 There flows a binding tar;
 The Holy Spirit fills the whole
 With strengthening, joining power.

5 These rafts of friendship make
 Christ's body here on earth;
 This mystic form in human shape
 Can bear us to new birth.

Words and Music © Copyright 2006 Stainer & Bell Ltd

A hymn written in November 1992 for a liturgy of the Catholic Women's Network, to whom I owe so much. It was a gift for Alexina Murphy as a thanksgiving at the time of her leaving Britain to live abroad. The words may also be sung to SANDYS, or any other appropriate tune in short metre.

4 Heaven

1 A thousand sacred harps,
   A hundred hymns of love –
   Will these be sounding in the place
   We call 'the heaven above'?

2 And will our friends be there
   With joyful welcome meals?
   Will they sing songs we all can share
   Filled with a balm that heals?

3 Is it a place of peace?
   Or just a place of rest
   Where energy can be renewed
   And we can feel more blessed?

4 Perhaps we shall still work
   To set the cosmos free;
   And justice still will lead us on
   To work for liberty.

5 An echo lingers here
   Of an eternal song;
   We sometimes catch the shining of
   The place where we belong –

6 A place that brings us hope,
   A sense of loving care
   Where we can catch a glimpse of God
   That leads us into prayer.

7 This tiny seed is hid
   Within each human hour
   And suddenly can leap to life
   And make our blessings shower.

8 We thank you for such gifts
   That make us feel beloved.
   May we live true to this on earth,
   Not wait till heaven above.

This was written at Prasada in response to a challenge to write a hymn about heaven. It can be sung to SANDYS or any short-metre tune like ALEXINA (see facing page).

Metre: SM

5   A Woman in her Grief

NETLEY MARSH   6.6.8.7.   *June Boyce-Tillman (1943–)*

A wo-man in her grief With-in a gar-den cried,

Lost in sense of deep be-reave-ment For the man she loved had died.

1 A woman in her grief
   Within a garden cried,
   Lost in sense of deep bereavement
   For the man she loved had died.

2 She wandered through the paths
   To search out where he lay,
   In devotion, bringing spices
   Her great debt to him to pay.

3 A man in working clothes
   Was also in that place,
   But her loss was overwhelming
   And she did not know his face.

4 He gently said one word:
   He called her by her name.
   It was just the sound she longed for
   And her heart was set aflame.

5 She recognised her love
   Who told her not to stay;
   So she left her contemplation
   For the world of everyday.

6 At times, God, you seem close
   But help us not to cling.
   May such ecstasy be harnessed
   For the world's transfiguring.

This was written on a train in May 1987 and was one of my earliest hymns. The tune title is taken from Netley Marsh churchyard in the New Forest where my grandparents are buried. One of my clearest childhood memories is of the visits that my mother and I made there every week. It reflects not only the grief of these occasions but also the contemplative way that has been central to my life. For this I owe a debt of gratitude to the Society of Friends through my long-standing friendship with Marian Liebmann and also the Rev. Canon Gonville ffrench-Beytagh who guided the practice for some twelve years. It has also been enriched by journeys in the area of interfaith dialogue.

6   A Julian Hymn

1   'All shall be well, in love enclosed,'
An anchoress says in her cell.
Her revelations clearly tell
Of love that lives in heaven and hell.

2   All shall be well, in love enclosed.
A God of judgement stands condemned
By One who only love can send,
Whose breath can heal, whose touch can mend.

3   All shall be well, in love enclosed
By One who holds us in his palm,
Who made us, shields us with his arm,
Redeems us, keeps us from all harm.

4   All shall be well, in love enclosed.
The ring of fire will meet the rose
In One who all our suffering knows,
Sweet Mother Jesus, our repose.

I have learned much from Julian of Norwich's 'Revelations of Divine Love'. This hymn, to be sung to GONFALON ROYAL or any other appropriate long-metre tune, was first sung in Westminster Abbey in September 1991 as part of a service led by Sister Hilary CSMV, on the subject of 'The Fire and the Rose' embroidered on the Abbey frontal. It was a time when I was exploring clowning in worship with a group called The Holy Fools. I developed two clown characters; the first was called 'Isabella', a silent whiteface (see Nos. 104 and 111), and the second 'Flombow'. He is a cocky fireman clown with large red boots, and he met with 'Rosie', alias Sister Lorna CSMV, who was also part of The Holy Fools.

Metre: LM

7 Women's Ordination

1 As Christ's body we move forward
   In the God who sets us free.
   Hoping, longing, weaving, struggling
   With outrageous liberty.
   Bread of heaven, bread of heaven,
   Feed us on the stony road.

2 Truth now leads us into action
   For the wounded of the earth.
   We would comfort, we would protest,
   Labouring in the world's rebirth.
   Oil of healing, oil of healing,
   Smooth the hands that soothe the world.

3 God of Wisdom's shaded pathway,
   Guide our faith communities,
   Shape our dreams, inspire our dancing
   With love's generosity.
   Songs of praises, songs of praises,
   Channel God's strong greening power.

At the celebration in St Martin-in-the-Fields held in November 1992 for the vote for women's ordination in the Church of England the King Alfred Singers performed one of the Magnificat Project pieces, by Julia Usher (see page xvii). This hymn, written for the occasion, was also sung, to CWM RHONDDA.

Metre: 8.7.8.7.8.7.

8   The Journey

1   Beauty for ever new,
    Kindling afresh like fire,
    Lasting eternally,
    You will not ever fail;
    A fervent flame without an end,
    Through all degrees of heaven you burn.

2   Nothing in heaven and earth
    Kindles so great a love,
    Settles such unquiet souls,
    Strengthens us where we are.
    Illimitable God you are,
    Perfection of the earth and heaven.

3   Yonder an endless song,
    Yonder an endless praise,
    Yonder no memories
    Of any troubled past,
    A ceaseless praise, the praise of God
    Is echoing through the heavenly spheres.

4   Yonder begins the song.
    Yonder begins the praise.
    Yet at the present time
    This is the pilgrim's joy.
    For part of human journeying
    Is beauty's everlasting song.

My earliest attempts at hymn writing were based on Celtic sources, with the idea that if these were fitted to well-known tunes the riches of the tradition might find their way into contemporary worship. This attempt, based on a text by William Williams (1716–91) was written in June 1988 in a Welsh farmhouse owned by Dr Helen Ford, who has performed miracles of healing for me. LITTLE CORNARD would be a suitable tune.

Metre: 6.6.6.6.8.8.

9 Ordination

CECILE   8.7.8.7.6 7.   *June Boyce-Tillman (1943–)*

Called to serve in our u-nique-ness, Shar-ing Christ's in - teg - ri - ty,___

We are firm in hope and long-ing For your spi - rit sets_ us free.___

Make_ our faith_ as_Christ's own_ For the call_ is yours a - lone.

For Sister Cecile CGA

1 Called to serve in our uniqueness,
   Sharing Christ's integrity,
   We are firm in hope and longing
   For your spirit sets us free.
   Make our faith as Christ's own
   For the call is yours alone.

2 Called to serve in holy Wisdom
   Channelling Christ's strengthening peace,
   We are true in joy and caring
   For your loving will not cease.
   Make our hearts as Christ's own
   For the call is yours alone.

3 Called to serve in desert places,
   Striking hard the rock of prayer,
   We are strong in faith and courage
   For your power is ours to share.
   Make our wills as Christ's own
   For the call is yours alone.

This text, written for the ordination of Sister Cecile CGA in Canterbury Cathedral in 1997, would also fit the well-known tune MICHAEL.

10 Resurrection Dance

HELSTON FLORAL DANCE

Katie Moss
arranged June Boyce-Tillman (1943–)

Christ - ians, to - ge - ther sing: 'Christ_ danc - es in our Re - sur - rec - tion Ring.'

Leap - ing here,___ fall - ing there, Danc - ing, laugh - ing__ ev - ery - where–

E - ven those with_ two left feet Can_ keep time with the Re - sur - rec - tion Beat.

danc - ing in the Re - sur - rec - tion Way.

1   Christians, together sing:
    'Christ dances in our Resurrection Ring.'
    Leaping here, falling there,
    Dancing, laughing everywhere –
    Even those with two left feet
    Can keep time with the Resurrection Beat.

2   Christians, now take a chance,
    Let go yourselves in Resurrection Dance.
    Meet your neighbour, give a shake,
    Pass right through and keep awake,
    Meet the next and give a hand,
    And keep time with the Resurrection Band.

3   Christians, now make a train
    And all join up in a Resurrection Chain.
    Put your hand around each waist,
    Don't draw back – come on! Make haste!
    Call your friends to come and play,
    All dancing in the Resurrection Way.

Version for dancing:

    Let us together sing:
    'Christ dances in our Resurrection Ring.'
    Heel and toe, sing merry, merry-o,
    Heel and toe, sing merry, merry-o,
    Heel and toe, sing merry, merry-o,
    Christ dances in our Resurrection Ring.

In 1990 Lala Winkley commissioned Resurrection Dance for a service to celebrate the birth of the new ecumenical organisation including Roman Catholics, 'Churches Together'. It was to be sung at what was intended as an ecumenical picnic outside the Imperial War Museum in Lambeth. Due to bad weather we ended up squashed in a local church hall. Nevertheless, we danced this in a procession (including several bishops) around the local streets. The dancing version has been used on Sutton Bank for sunrise on Easter morning in 2005, and for a garden dance at the opening of Hexthorpe Manor, Doncaster in May 2006 (see No. 33).

11 The Risen Christ

1 Christ, our companion, gloriously alive,
   We can share your darkness, we can share your life.
   In the rocky cavern, dead your body lay,
   Till the shining angels rolled the stone away.
   Christ, our companion, gloriously alive,
   We can share your darkness, we can share your life.

2 Risen in glory, Christ still meets us here,
   Lovingly enfolds us, quietens our fear.
   So the faithful household sings the joyful hymn:
   'Grief can't last for ever; death has lost its sting.'
   Chorus

3 Christ's glorious living is for us to share.
   Lost in adoration, trust will be our prayer.
   Help us through the darkness, lead us through the night,
   Guarding deep within us, visions of the light.
   Chorus

On behalf of the Movement for the Ordination of Women, Caroline Davies commissioned this new paraphrase of the original French text by Edmond Budry (1854–1932) for the memorial service to commemorate the life of the Chinese woman priest, Lee Tim Oi, that was held at St Martin-in-the-Fields in June 1992. These words balance the triumphalism of the more familiar translation 'Thine be the glory' and see the Passion and Resurrection story as a balance of light and darkness. We have both in our lives and the story shows Christ in them both. To be sung to Handel's MACCABEUS.

Metre: 10 11.11 11. and Chorus 10 11.

12 Jesus who is called Christ

SOPHIA   *June Boyce-Tillman (1943–)*

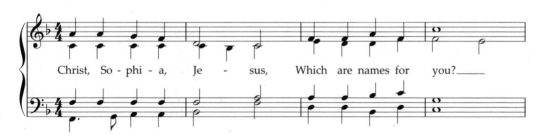

Christ, So - phi - a,   Je - sus,   Which are names for   you?____

Christ, So - phi - a,   Je - sus,____   Make___ all things new.

1 Christ, Sophia, Jesus,
   Which are names for you?
   Christ, Sophia, Jesus,
   Make all things new.

2 Christ, Sophia, Jesus,
   Which name is mine,
   As I taste your presence
   In bread and wine?

3 Christ, Sophia, Jesus,
   Earth is your name,
   Rooted deep within you,
   All bloom again.

4 Christ, Sophia, Jesus,
   You stand outside,
   Peering through the barred gates,
   Access denied.

5 Christ, Sophia, Jesus,
   I would name you too,
   Name you in a life that
   Makes all things new.

6 Christ, Sophia, Jesus,
   All bear your name,
   Mystic, Christic body,
   Love's erotic flame.

The last lecture of Professor Carter Heyward's Christology module in 2003 at the Episcopal Divinity School, Cambridge, Massachusetts, USA was a liturgy in which we were asked to create something that reflected the module. In ten minutes I had completed this, so powerful was her teaching. I spent three months as Proctor Scholar at the Divinity School under the guidance of Professor Kwok Pui Lan in a transforming experience. I also visited Carter's inspiring community in North Carolina.

13 Advent

MONICA SM

June Boyce-Tillman (1943–)

1 Come, our Emanuel,
The God who sets us free,
Help us to live abundantly,
Find our true destiny.

2 Come, regal, roaring lion,
Create our world again;
Move in our vulnerable hearts;
Be gentle with our pain.

3 Come, wounded, healing hands,
And soothe our flesh with balm;
Enfold the universe with strength,
Holding its storms with calm.

4 Come, ancient David's key,
   Shut doors that need to close;
   Unlock the hidden springs of love
   So that our mercy flows.

5 Come, Israel's Adonai,
   With burning bushy fuel,
   Sweep all the bitterness away
   And etch in us your rule.

6 Come, branch of Jesse's tree,
   Make sure our wood is green.
   Lone woman, bear your child with strength,
   For us God's go-between.

7 Come, Wisdom's child, in play
   Our loveliness enhance,
   Transform our earthbound, ageing steps
   Into a youthful dance.

I wrote this hymn on 20 September 1992, the day when my eldest son, Matthew, left home for university. It draws on my thinking on the Advent antiphons, which has been greatly enriched by the Cries of Advent meditation cards published by the Rev. Jim Cotter's press, Cairns Publications. It was first sung at an Advent meeting of the Wimbledon Liturgy Group. The tune is named after Monica Furlong (see No. 17), but any appropriate short-metre tune, such as SOUTHWELL, could also be used.

14　A Hymn for Mothering Sunday

1　Deep growing freshness in the earth
　Is making all things new;
　Such greening force is God's own truth,
　Creation flowing through.
　We sense a warmth, a loving touch,
　Our greening is affirmed.

2　The broken-hearted shed those tears
　That wipe away the pain.
　There is a balm in nature's heart
　And family and friends.
　Chorus

3　Joy bubbles up in youthful hearts,
　Birds sing, the sea is warm;
　Deep in community we find
　God's love in human form.
　Chorus

4　Mothering strength is drawn from God,
　Deep in creation's heart;
　Let us give thanks for those in whom
　Our human living starts.
　Chorus

A stay in New Zealand with my very good friends Stuart and Margaret Manins inspired 'A Hymn for Mothering Sunday'. The word 'greening' in the chorus draws on Hildegard's idea of 'viriditas' – a greening power that runs through all creation. It was written in February 1995 for the Rev. Elizabeth Baxter who, with her husband Stanley, runs Holy Rood House in Sowerby, Yorkshire. The tune is BROTHER JAMES' AIR.

Metre: 8.6.8.6. and Chorus 8.6.

15 Cosmic Eucharist

ANDREW   8.7.8.7.

June Boyce-Tillman (1943–)

Deep in - side_ cre - a - tion's_mys-tery Stands a ta - ble set_ with bread,

And a cup of_ grapes' re - joic-ing, Love full - bo - died,_ spark-ling_ red._

1 Deep inside creation's mystery
   Stands a table set with bread,
   And a cup of grapes' rejoicing,
   Love full-bodied, sparkling red.

2 Hands reach out across the cosmos;
   Each is gladly taking part,
   Offering deeply all their being
   In this Eucharistic heart.

3 Rocks and stones rejoice together;
   Insects, birds can join the song;
   Flowers leap up and clouds are dancing;
   All are joined and all are strong.

4 Human voices join the chorus;
   Chant and jazz and mystic prose,
   Hymns of fellowship all make the
   Counterpoint of One who Knows.

5 Life-transforming celebration
   Centring eccentricity,
   Shape our dancing, keep it rooted
   In love's creativity.

6 We all bear the marks of loving
   In our hearts. That is the plan.
   In our own truth we shall find that
   Truth, in whom we all began.

This was written originally in Winchester in June 1994 but revised at the Abtei St Hildegard in Bingen in September of that year. It was a present for the Rev. Andrew Todd, the chaplain of King Alfred's College of Higher Education, when he left. It summarises a lot of my discussions with him over his three years as chaplain and his involvement with Franciscan spirituality. Since then as Canon Andrew Todd he has been alongside a great deal of my spiritual journey, especially that part of it leading to ordination. It also reflects my deep gratitude for all that he taught me. It was first sung at a Eucharist celebrated in a field near my childhood home. The tune, bearing his name, was written while walking among vines which were heavy with the grape harvest. CROSS OF JESUS may also be used as a traditional alternative.

16 A Prayer for Wisdom

For Patricia Naylor

1 Deep within us God is holy,
   Wisdom planted in the dark.
   We are dreaming, searching slowly;
   Softly will our journey start.

2 Deep within a seed is growing;
   Petals form the flower head.
   Beauty lights the path that's flowing
   Through the dried-up riverbed.

3 In the shimmering we are listening
   To the fruitful voice within;
   In our waiting, in our glistening,
   Truthful living can begin.

The allusions in this text (written as a birthday present) to shimmering and glistening are to the 'shekinah', the radiant glory of God, referred to in the Old Testament. CROSS OF JESUS will fit these words. Patricia Naylor, then at St Anne's, Lambeth, offered me a great deal of support when I first came to London in 1966 to study for a PGCE. I lived then in Bickersteth House in Sheffield Terrace, but went to Pat and her welcoming family for Sunday lunch.

Metre: 8.7.8.7.

17 Grief

1 Fall, fall those healing tears,
    Pour salt upon the pain,
    Cleanse all that will infect the wound,
    Restore my life again.

2 Pour, pour that healing salve,
    Anoint my weary feet;
    Long is the journey I must make
    And scorching is the heat.

3 Bathe, bathe my aching heart
    With gently soothing balm;
    Sharp are the wounds that love can bring,
    Incurable the harm.

4 Wrap, wrap the body tight
    And lay it in the tomb;
    Close round me falls the enfolding night,
    The darkness of the womb.

5 Rise, rise my joyful heart,
    The wounds are nearly healed,
    Take once again the heavenward road,
    Cleansed scars will be your shield.

This hymn and the tune MONICA (see No. 13) were written in September 1992 as a present for my good friend Monica Furlong, who gave me such encouragement. We met to share ideas and to help her lead singing at the St Hilda Community. Her stammer (like the stammers of many other people) disappeared when she sang. The words reflect my own experience of grief and the healing of wounds caused by an electrical accident. The tune is intended to remind singers of the tune for 'Drop, drop, slow tears' – Orlando Gibbons's SONG 46. The opening of the tune is a minor version of Gibbons's first bar and the harmony of the end with the dissonance in the bass resembles the discord at the beginning of the second bar in SONG 46. The original text by Phineas Fletcher refers to the believer's tears falling in contrition for sin. My text links this with human woundedness and vulnerability and the stages of grieving.

Metre: SM

18 Hymn for Hild of Whitby

JEAN   8.7.8.7.   *June Boyce-Tillman (1943–)*

Em - brace the un - i - verse with love, And shine with God___ in splen - dour; Em - brace the earth, em - brace___ the sky And find God, our de - fen - der.

For Jean Mayland

1 Embrace the universe with love,
   And shine with God in splendour;
   Embrace the earth, embrace the sky
   And find God, our defender.

2 Find Wisdom hidden in the stars
   And faith within the rainbow.
   Find righteousness in flowing streams
   And hope in moon and meadow.

3   Embrace your friend, embrace your foe,
    And find the Christ within them;
    Embrace your body and your mind;
    These also are God-given.

4   For mercy dwells in human hearts
    And needs our love to shape it.
    Put out a hand and touch a heart
    And help to consecrate it.

5   Share all you have with all you meet
    And find the strength of Scripture;
    Prepare the heart, prepare the mind
    And leave to God the future.

6   And so a death with joy and peace
    Will be Christ's benediction.
    Creator God, we sing your praise,
    Like Hild, we seek your vision.

This was written for the dedication of the St Hild icon in Durham Cathedral in 1999. It draws on the Venerable Bede's account of Hild's death. St Hild is better known as St Hilda. The Bede added the 'a' to the Celtic name Hild in order to integrate it into his Latin text. The hymn forms part of my one-woman performance 'Celtic Twilight – St Hild of Whitby'. This uses dance, song and storytelling to explore the meeting of the Celtic traditions with Roman Christianity, and links this with current dialogues between Christianity and the so-called New Age. The tune is dedicated to my friend, the Rev. Jean Mayland, who has supported my journey. ST COLUMBA may be used as an alternative tune.

19 Firmly We Believe and Truly

1 Firmly we believe and truly
   God created heaven and earth;
   And we next acknowledge duly
   Mary gave that Wisdom birth.

2 And we trust and hope most fully
   That God acts within our pain,
   Labouring lovingly and deeply
   Till our life is birthed again.

3 We can sense the Holy Spirit
   Struggling here creatively
   Everywhere and every minute
   For the earth's integrity.

4 We seek reconciliation
   In a world that longs for peace;
   We will work for resurrection
   With God's joy that brings release.

5 Glory be to God Creator,
   Who transforms our living here,
   And the Spirit, our Sustainer
   Always strengthening, always near.

6 Adoration now be given
   In and through the angel throng
   To the God of earth and heaven
   Through the earth's symphonic song.

This was written in response to a BBC request for new creedal statements. It is a reworking of Cardinal Newman's hymn 'Firmly I believe and truly', with echoes of that text clearly present (for example, in verse six). It is designed to be sung to SHIPSTON, the tune usually associated with the Newman text.

Metre: 8.7.8.7.

20 Flame of Love

FLAME OF LOVE   8.7.8.7.   *June Boyce-Tillman (1943–)*

1 Flame of fire from midmost heaven,
   Come down freely to our world;
   Set on fire our stubborn natures;
   You'll not fail while God prevails.

2 And despite our greatest efforts
   There is none that can compare
   With the sweetness and the power
   Of the endless flame of love.

3 You have kindled fire within us
   Fervent fire from midmost heaven.
   All the great seas cannot quench it,
   Nor the fountains' leaping dance.

4 Fire of strength and fire of passion
   Kindled deep in midmost heaven,
   Everlasting love that's burning
   And uniting God with us.

The words are adapted from a Celtic source, and may also be sung to LOVE DIVINE. The tune FLAME OF LOVE was written for my one-woman performance 'Celtic Twilight – St Hild of Whitby' (see No. 18).

21 Flourishing Branch

GELOBT SEI GOTT
8 8 8 and Alleluias

*Melody from Melchior Vulpius's Gesangbuch 1609
harmonised June Boyce-Tillman (1943–)*

Flou-rish-ing branch, you bear rich fruit, An-swer tra - di - tion's quest for truth. New life that springs from an-cient roots. Al - le - lu - ia, al - le - lu - ia, al - le - lu - ia.

1 Flourishing branch, you bear rich fruit,
   Answer tradition's quest for truth.
   New life that springs from ancient roots.
   Alleluia, alleluia, alleluia.
   (Or *Ave Maria, Ave Maria, Alleluia.*)

2 Warmth of the sun distilled in you,
   Glows and makes fragrant blossoms new,
   Balsam and rose and dusky rue.
   Alleluia, alleluia, alleluia.

3 Skies drop their dew on rolling fields;
    Deep in your womb the dark earth yields;
    Sheltering nests their fledglings shield.
    Alleluia, alleluia, alleluia.

4 Fine is the flower that grows in you,
    Dryness is ended, earth made new.
    God's creativity breaks through.
    Alleluia, alleluia, alleluia.

5 Your greening power has borne rich fruit;
    From a fine trunk new branches shoot;
    Firmly they stand on ancient roots.
    Alleluia, alleluia, alleluia.

6 Earth is rejoicing, now made new;
    Blossoming power is flowing through;
    Paradise visions come in view.
    Alleluia, alleluia, alleluia.

7 Eve's condemnation filled these things;
    Joy is the gift that Mary brings;
    So through eternity we'll sing;
    Alleluia, alleluia, alleluia.

For the Hildegard conference in April 1995 at King Alfred's College, Winchester entitled 'Greening Love', I wrote this paraphrase of Hildegard's hymn 'O viridissima virga'. The use of the tune (which was my father's favourite) gives it an Easter character and emphasises Hildegard's use of new-life imagery in the context of Mary. The choice of two choruses gives the potential for making the relationship with Mary clear. The last verse can be deleted and the Alleluias chosen; then it becomes a hymn giving thanks for the Easter theme of resurrection in the spring. The arrangement is for unison singing but it may be sung in four parts with suitable rhythmic adjustment of the lower voices. A long-standing friend of mine, Mary Gordon, has illustrated clearly the greening power in her 'greening days' that she holds regularly in Kendal and in which I have participated. These explore a variety of ways of healing and spirituality.

22   A Hymn for St Augustine's Day

June Boyce-Tillman (1943–)

For Sister Jean CGA

1 God most beautiful, most mighty,
  Merciful, yet just and strong,
  Hidden, yet eternally present,
  Changing things, not old nor young,
  Nourish and create, perfect us,
  For it is to you we belong.

2 You pay debts and yet owe nothing,
  Cancel debts and do not grow poor;
  Payments made to you are excessive,
  So your debt to us grows more;
  And yet how can we possess now
  Anything that is not yours.

3 Angry, without losing your quiet,
  Active, yet at rest you stand,
  You are full of love, yet centred,
  Change your works but not your plan.
  Still our hearts, for we are restless
  And our rest lies in your hand.

Words and Music © Copyright 2006 Stainer & Bell Ltd

The tune PICARDY might also be a suitable accompaniment for this text, written at Prasada, in Montauroux, France, for St Augustine's Day, 2001, and paraphrasing verses from St Augustine's Confessions.

23 Empowerment

For Rev. David Page and Brenda Harrison

1 God of empowerment, spiralling Wisdom,
   Gently reshaping life's myriad forms,
   Bless all relationships worked in your loving,
   Challenge a culture's imprisoning norms.
   God of empowerment, God of diversity,
   Holding the cosmos in strengthening embrace,
   Sure that we fit in your rainbow mosaic,
   We will live boldly through inclusive grace.

2 God of empowerment, Jesus expressed you;
   He scanned the margins to find the reviled,
   Honoured their insight and shared in their weeping,
   Showed how your image is in the exiled.
   Chorus

3 God of empowerment, we seek your Wisdom,
   Trust your integrity at work inside,
   Showing your faithfulness, marking your justice,
   We will walk bravely for yours is the pride.
   Chorus

For the service in St Martin-in-the-Fields when Gene Robinson, Bishop of Massachusetts, visited the United Kingdom, in November 2005, and written in response to a request from Changing Attitudes. I chose the tune FAITHFULNESS as I believe in God's faithfulness to all people, not just those of a particular sexual orientation. There are hints of the original text in verse three as well as suggestions of the celebration of the Gay Pride marches. It also sees that the real vice is arrogance, not pride. In verse two, the slight mismatch of the stress of the word 'exiled' with the tune is intentional, to show how the marginalised often have difficulty fitting with the dominant culture.

Metre: 11.10.11.10. and Chorus 12.10.11.10.

24 Millennium Hymn

HILDEGARD 8.7.8.7.D.

June Boyce-Tillman (1943–)

God of jus - tice, wind the cir - cle, Mak - ing all the cos - mos one;

Show us in mil - len - nial vi - sions, How on earth your will__ is done;

Help us see the mer - cy flow - ing From the wound-ing of__Christ's side;

Heal us with com-pas - sion spread-ing As a pu - ri - fy - ing tide.

1 God of justice, wind the circle,
Making all the cosmos one;
Show us in millennial visions,
How on earth your will is done;
Help us see the mercy flowing
From the wounding of Christ's side;
Heal us with compassion spreading
As a purifying tide.

2 God of dreams and intuition,
   Inspiration from the night,
   Temper reason's rigid systems
   With the leap of faith's insight.
   God of passion, fill our knowing
   With divine authority,
   And a sense of mystery leading
   To a right humility.

3 God of faith's heroic journey,
   May your truth direct our way;
   Guide our footsteps, give us courage
   In the challenge of each day.
   God of Wisdom's spinning spiral,
   Soothe us with your gentle charms,
   Weave our lives into the pattern
   Of Christ's all-embracing arms.

4 God of order, God of chaos,
   In love's creativity
   Move the mountains of tradition,
   Stifling earth's fertility:
   Break the barriers, guide the learning,
   Bind the wounds and heal the pain,
   Bring to birth our human yearning,
   Integrate the world again.

This hymn, written for the millennium, encompasses the thinking that underpins my book 'Constructing Musical Healing: The Wounds that Sing' (Jessica Kingsley Publishers, 2000). It concerns the need for balance in our own lives and our theology and was first tried out with Myra Poole SND. It sees the need for a balance between intuition and reason, linear journeys and encircling Wisdom and order and chaos. However, its attempt to do this resulted in its failure to find ready acceptance in some churches. The tune was first sung to Michael Finnissy, whose encouragement has been so important to me. In its choral version it was premiered on 11 October 1998 in St Mary de Haura, New Shoreham, West Sussex by Philip Adams's choir. ABBOT'S LEIGH would make a suitable alternative tune for this text.

25 Confirmation

1 God of spirit's fiery flaming,
   Burn our hearts and give us peace.
   All we ask is your acceptance,
   And a love that will not cease.
   To be born here on earth
   Was a greater, mightier wonder.

2 You it is who makes the brightness,
   You it is who freezes ice.
   You it is who fills the river,
   Keeps the salmon in its depths.
   In your love, all is held,
   What a miracle is greater?

3 In your hand the fruit tree flowers,
   In your hand the kernel forms.
   In your hand the young wheat springs up
   And the ear of corn is born.
   Skilled your hands in such craft.
   Who can fathom such a wonder?

4 You it is who to redeem us
   Entered into human pain;
   Like a metal in a furnace
   You were molten and refined.
   You sustain nature's life;
   Feed the flame of love within us.

5 You, creator, hang transfigured
   On a cross of burning hate,
   Showing us in painful passion
   Unsuspected depths in love.
   Mary's child, born of earth,
   Make our dying, your creation.

6 Soon will come the great awakening,
   Now the rending of the tomb,
   Soon the end of anxious weeping,
   Now the piercing of the gloom.
   Risen Christ, in each heart,
   Leap up in the spirit's flaming.

With the tune MICHAEL in mind, I wrote this hymn using ideas from Celtic sources, for the confirmation of my youngest son, Richard, in May 1987 by Ronald Bowlby, then Bishop of Southwark, at St Paul's Church, Tooting. It has echoes of other hymn texts learned from my childhood, such as 'Through the night of doubt and sorrow'. Verse five sees the relationship between living and dying, and that death can be a source of new life. In setting these words to such a strong tune, I hope that the power of the original text, 'All my hope on God is founded', will also reverberate in the hearts of the singers.

Metre: 8.7.8.7.6.8.

1 Greenness dancing in the earth
Brings about the world's rebirth.
This is God's vitality
Join the dance and set it free.

2 Shared responsibility
Forms the world's ecology.
Chorus

3 Partnership within the dance
Will God's turning shapes enhance.
Chorus

4 Through God's generosity
Nature gives abundantly.
Chorus

5 Giving ourselves prayerfully
Shapes celestial energy.
Chorus

6 Bringing our gifts joyfully
Shares God's creativity.
Chorus

This was a commission from the Christian Stewardship Campaign in January 1999. The tune is MONKLAND, and any performance should reflect the dance-like character of the text, which would indeed lend itself to dancing. There is the notion here of Hildegard's 'greening power' that enlivens all creation. It sees us as partners in divine creativity, drawing on Mechtild of Magdeburg's idea of God as our dancing partner.

Metre: 7 7. and Chorus 7 7.

27 Hildegard

PICARDY   8.7.8.7.8.7.

*Traditional French
arranged June Boyce-Tillman (1943–)*

Hil - de - gard of faith un - bend - ing, Fea - ther on the breath of___ God, World of sub-stance all trans - cend - ing, Tread-ing paths as yet un - trod, In dis-cern-ment tra - velled for - - ward, Pe - ne - trat-ing Wis - dom's knot.

1 Hildegard of faith unbending,
   Feather on the breath of God,
   World of substance all transcending,
   Treading paths as yet untrod,
   In discernment travelled forward,
   Penetrating Wisdom's knot.

2 Lonely woman, silence keeping
   Till the time to speak came near,
   Then the praise of God unceasing
   From your lips the world could hear,
   Justice for a whole creation
   Underpinned your message clear.

3 May discernment bring us wisdom.
   In compassion may we love.
   Deep in joy may we find laughter.
   May our trust be just enough,
   So that, dancing, we may enter
   Shining courts in heaven above.

This was originally written for the first of the evenings with Hildegard of Bingen organised by Ianthe Pratt for the Association for Inclusive Language in March 1991. It now forms part of the meditation I devised, which uses the music and words of this remarkable medieval mystic as well as my own piano pieces. It was originally written for the plainchant melody PANGE LINGUA, as being a tune in use today that is quite close to the style used by Hildegard herself. For Roman Catholics, this tune was seen to represent the more conservative theology that pre-dated the Second Vatican Council, and would therefore not be readily acceptable to more radical, progressive Roman Catholics. The story shows how particular musical styles are associated with particular theological positions.

Urban Spirit

AD PERENNIS VITAE FONTEM
8.7.8.7.8.7. trochaic

Ad Perennis Vitae Fontem, Tours Breviary (1781)
arranged June Boyce-Tillman (1943–)

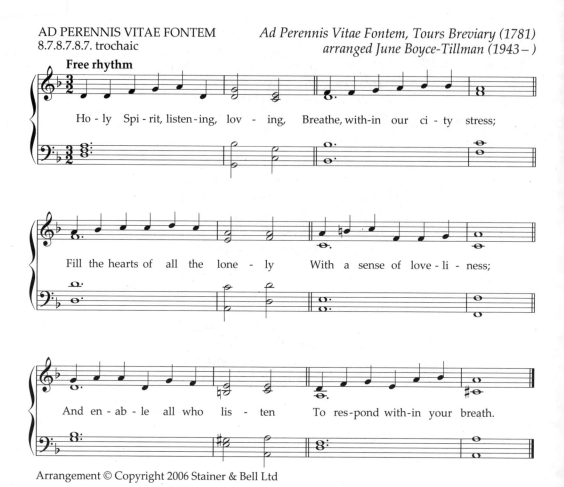

1 Holy Spirit, listening, loving,
   Breathe within our city stress;
   Fill the hearts of all the lonely
   With a sense of loveliness;
   And enable all who listen
   To respond within your breath.

2 Holy Spirit, caring, sharing,
   Warm the anonymity;
   Make of labyrinthine mazes
   Patterns of community;
   And enable all the caring
   To respond within your warmth.

3 Holy Spirit, washing, cleansing,
   Flow among our city streets;
   Purify the trace of evil,
   Cleanse the structures of disease;
   And enable all reformers
   To respond within your flow.

4 Holy Spirit, driving, powerful,
   Blow around our city towers,
   Guide the strong, support the weakened
   And direct the path of power;
   And enable all who govern
   To respond within your strength.

5 Holy Spirit, singing, leaping,
   Set on fire our city's heart;
   Make of vibrant celebrations
   A pulsating, dancing art;
   And enable all creators
   To respond within your fire.

This was written on a train in July 1987 after a Hymn Society conference in which a speaker had talked of the difficulty of writing hymns for an urban community. It is the first of my hymns exploring the elements as images for the Holy Spirit. The use of an arrangement of a melody from the Tours Breviary reflects my enthusiasm for a greater use of plainchant in contemporary worship.

29 Thanksgiving for a Holiday

PERTH

June Boyce-Tillman (1943–)

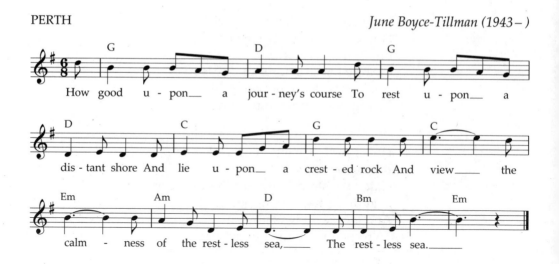

How good u-pon__ a jour-ney's course To rest u-pon__ a
dis-tant shore And lie u-pon__ a crest-ed rock And view____ the
calm - ness of the rest-less sea,___ The rest-less sea.____

2 And hear the ocean's mighty waves
  Upon the glittering silver sea
  In chants of everlasting praise
  To God, their maker and sustainer,
  Their sustainer here.

3 And see its ebb and floodtide flow
  Upon the sparkling silver sands
  And hear it calling out the name
  Of one who travelled far yet will return,
  Yet will return.

4 And bless the power in it all,
  The One who keeps the swelling waves,
  The crystal angels of the heavens,
  The earth, the ebbing and the flowing tide,
  The flowing tide.

5 And so a soul will be renewed
  And drink from ocean's welling depths,
  Return again to homely shores
  In contemplation of the tide of love,
  The tide of love.

This text, based on one by St Columba, was written while watching the waves of the Indian Ocean breaking on the shore at Perth, during a lecture tour to Australia in August 1988, at a time of great change for me. It may also be sung to ST MARGARET (Peace).

30 For the Dedication of a Crib

1 In dulci jubilo,
  Let love within us glow;
  See the Christ child lying
  Within praesepio,
  Who shares our joy and crying,
  Matris in gremio.
  Alpha es et O.

2 O patris caritas!
  O nati lenitas!
  We were told we're guilty
  Per nostra crimina;
  But we were birthed in beauty –
  Coelorum gaudia.
  Our own births were blessed.

3 Ubi sunt gaudia?
  But here with human friends;
  We hear angels singing
  Nova cantica;
  With these songs are mingling
  In regis curia.
  We can share that joy.

This was written for the dedication of the crib at Ianthe Pratt's house in December 2003. It was a lovely ceremony conducted largely in the darkness on Christmas Eve. The hymn retains the macaronic (two-language) character of the original text in the form of the Latin lines. 'Per nostra crimina' gave me a problem, but I have reworked it in line with a theology of original blessing, not sin. It also sees heaven as situated not in some future life but in gatherings of friends here and now, such as those that regularly gather in Ianthe's beautiful house and garden. The translations of the Latin are:

In dulci jubilo	*In sweet rejoicing*
praesepio	*cradle*
Matris in gremio	*In his mother's lap*
O patris caritas!	*O God's love of the father!*
O nati lenitas!	*O gentleness of the son!*
Per nostra crimina	*Because of our sins*
Coelorum gaudia	*The joys of heaven*
Ubi sunt gaudia?	*Where are the joys?*
Nova cantica	*New songs*
In regis curia	*In the chamber of the king*

31   Harvest of Darkness

HARVEST OF DARKNESS

June Boyce-Tillman (1943–)
with chorus from Millicent Kingham (1866–1894)

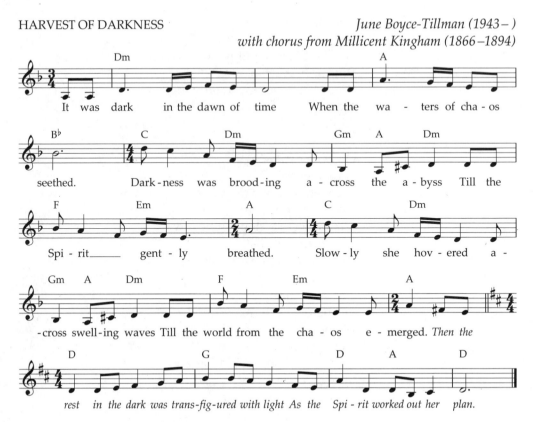

It was dark in the dawn of time When the wa - ters of cha - os
seethed. Dark - ness was brood - ing a - cross the a - byss Till the
Spi - rit_____ gent - ly breathed. Slow - ly she hov - ered a -
- cross swell - ing waves Till the world from the cha - os e - merged. *Then the*
rest in the dark was trans-fig-ured with light As the Spi - rit worked out her plan.

1   It was dark in the dawn of time
    When the waters of chaos seethed.
    Darkness was brooding across the abyss
    Till the Spirit gently breathed.
    Slowly she hovered across swelling waves
    Till the world from the chaos emerged.
    Then the rest in the dark was transfigured with light
    As the Spirit worked out her plan.

2   It was dark in the rocky cave
    Where the body of Jesus lay.
    Resting down deep in the heart of the earth
    Till the stone was rolled away.
    In the still night he'd stayed hidden away
    In the cold of primeval gloom.
    Chorus

3 Mary sank down deep into grief
    When her master was crucified.
    Deep in the darkness of sadness she lay
    Till her love she recognised.
    Waiting she stayed all alone in the night
    In the chaos of loss and despair.
    Chorus

4 It is dark in the moistened earth
    Where the seed for a season lies
    Buried down deep as a dry pregnant husk
    Till the earth is pushed aside.
    Nurtured by warmth, it has waited alone
    Till the time to spring up has come.
    Chorus

5 It is dark in the sheltering womb
    Where the baby for nine months lies,
    Curved like a moon near a warm woman's heart
    Till the waters roll aside.
    Waters of life kept the child safe inside
    Gently folded, enclosed in love.
    Chorus

6 It is dark in the heart's deep cells
    Where the Spirit of Wisdom lies.
    Firm are the strong rooms and bars of the mind
    Till the barriers are rolled aside.
    Yet her idea in the dark has been formed
    Till the time for release should come.
    Chorus

This was written for a BBC hymn contest in 1991, as an effort to redeem the darkness and to present the Holy Spirit as feminine, in line with feminist theologians such as Rosemary Radford Ruether. It may also be sung to BENSON, from which the chorus is taken. It is used as part of the opening of my one-woman performance entitled 'Lunacy or the Pursuit of the Goddess', where the need for a regular descent into the underworld and chaos is explored.

32 Jubilee

1 Jubilee sets us free!
   Shout with a strong north wind,
   Bringer of dignity,
   Singer of freedom's hymn.
   Deep in the earth our God is strong
   And chants with love the captives' song.

2 Jubilee sets us free!
   Long for a sharp east wind,
   Guiding community
   Back to its origin.
   The air of God flows free and pure;
   Our trust grows firm, our hope is sure.

3 Jubilee sets us free!
   Weep with a soft west wind,
   Pleading for unity
   With foes and friends and kin.
   The tears of God flow far and wide,
   A reconciling, cleansing tide.

4 Jubilee sets us free!
   Dance in a hot south wind,
   Flaming creatively,
   Our fiery God within.
   With life renewed, we find our voice;
   Rise up with joy, in God rejoice.

This was written for a Eucharist for the Queen's Golden Jubilee held at Ianthe Pratt's house, and should be sung to LITTLE CORNARD. It uses the four parts of the compass as in the text 'Hills of the north rejoice', usually sung to this tune. Here the images of the winds are used as metaphors for characteristics of the biblical notion of a jubilee year, rather than the more imperialistic use of the compass points in the original. The compass points are also used in some traditions as invocations to create a sacred space. This has long been part of my prayer practice, and it enables me to orientate myself in relation to the natural world.

Metre: 6.6.6.6.8 8.

33 God as Lord – Loaf Giver and Hospitable Host

1 Loaf provider, wine fermenter
   Set the table for our feast,
   Plump the cushions, make a welcome
   For the greatest and the least;
   We would tap your flowing Wisdom
   And the richness of your peace.

2 Here we gather, here we draw on
   Your warm hospitality;
   May we gently face our problems
   In your creativity,
   Knowing that your arms are holding
   Our diverse community.

3 Guard our visions, shield our dreaming
   In the darkness of your womb;
   Float them gently on your waters,
   Nurture them and give them room
   So that when they come to birthing
   They will touch earth's deepest wounds.

This hymn was written for Hexthorpe Manor, which I helped to open in May 2006 alongside the Rt Rev. Jack Nicholls, Bishop of Sheffield. I used the tune WESTMINSTER ABBEY as 'Christ is made the sure foundation' was an appropriate underpin for the day. It is the favourite tune of Matthew Burnell, the house warden. Hexthorpe Manor, an extension of the work of Holy Rood, will house a transformative community for young people at turning points in their lives. It takes the meaning of lord as loaf provider, and in the sermon I talked to the children about the role of the lord of the manor. It sees God as an hospitable host who is interested in practical things like plumped-up cushions. These are part of the hospitality of this beautiful house. It celebrates inclusivity and the need for a safe place to bring dreams to fruition in God's creativity.

Metre: 8.7.8.7.8.7.

34 Let All the Stars in Heaven

NUN DANKET   6.7.6.7. and Chorus 6.6.6.6.

Melody from Praxis Pietatis Melica (1647)
arranged June Boyce-Tillman (1943–)

1 Let all the stars in heaven
   Sing out to God creator
   And use whatever sound
   Their various forms can utter.
   And we will praise a God
   That is beyond a name
   Who taking human form
   As son of Mary came.

2 We cannot tell what womb
   Within the encircling cosmos
   Is giving birth to God
   To make another Christmas.
   Chorus

3 We cannot tell what shapes
   Can hold our God's revealing
   But Jesus shared my flesh
   And that for me is healing.
   Chorus

4 We cannot tell what cross
   Today or in the future
   Or many moons ago
   Will bruise God-given nature.
   Chorus

5 Let galaxies rejoice
   And praise divine empowering
   The countless gifts of love
   Of generous God's enshowering.
   Chorus

I have been greatly influenced by Sydney Carter, but when I went to use 'Every star shall sing a carol' I found the non-inclusive language of the chorus 'God above, man below' impossible now; so this is a rework of the ideas. I wrote it at the end of the doctrine module of my ordination course. It reminded me that there are more answers than questions and that these are held in the mystery of God. When I sang this to my friend the Rt Rev. Prof. Elizabeth Stuart, she saw verse three especially as expressing the centrality of the incarnation to Christian certainty. The tune is the original secular version of NUN DANKET. Luther used secular tunes for his chorales, a decision immortalised in his words 'Why should the Devil have all the tunes?' They were gradually slowed down by harmonising every note. This version was originally used in the hymn book 'New Orbit' for primary schools (Galliard, 1972).

35 St Clare

PRASADA

June Boyce-Tillman (1943–)

Li - ly, rose and vio - let Shine in na-ture's lov - ing, Pure in hum-ble joy.

Flowers of mis - ty moun - tains, Lit by south - ern sun - light

Glow in rhyth - mic dance. Clare and Fran - cis laugh - ing there

Drew from Wis-dom's nat - ural life A - ve - nues of faith.

Lily, rose and violet
Shine in nature's loving,
Pure in humble joy.

1 Flowers of misty mountains,
  Lit by southern sunlight
  Glow in rhythmic dance.
  Clare and Francis laughing there
  Drew from Wisdom's natural life
  Avenues of faith.
  Chorus

2 Sunlit strength of noonday,
  Moonlit path at midnight,
  Energies of love
  Brought Clare's creativity
  Inspiration full of joy
  From creation's Source.
  Chorus

3 Planted in Clare's garden,
  These became her beauty
  Closed from worldly gaze,
  Symbols of a strengthened life,
  Poor in coins, but rich at heart,
  Channelling God's grace.
  Chorus

4 So may we in living
  Joy in our creating
  From Sophia's spring;
  And not fear to be ourselves
  Energised by freeing love,
  Wisdom's ancient strength.
  Chorus

This was written for a Eucharist celebrated by the Rev. Bridget Woollard at Prasada, the home of Sisters Cecile and Jean of the Community of the Glorious Ascension at Montauroux in Provence. The lily, rose and violet were grown by Clare, St Francis's sister, in her convent garden. I assumed that many ideas of Francis were Clare's as well. For the service in their beautiful glass-sided chapel, Bridget created a fine purple, white and pink flower arrangement. My holiday friend Pam Gladding and I have spent many happy holidays in the relaxing care of this house of peace. The tune bears the title of the house which is taken from 'prashad', the food that is part of the Hindu/ Sikh celebrations. The original tune was JESU MEINE FREUDE but it was considered too sombre for this text. Although the harmonic moves in the odd-numbered lines are complex, every even line returns to the same simple tune, like two children playing with ideas.

36 Mary, our Mother

BUNESSAN 10.9.10.9.

Gaelic Melody
arranged June Boyce-Tillman (1943 –)

Mary, our mo - ther, You are with - in us, Guard-ing, pro-tect - ing, Keep-ing us safe. Be with our wak - ing, Be with our sleep - ing, Fold-ing us round with Cir-cles of love.

1 Mary, our mother,
   You are within us,
   Guarding, protecting,
   Keeping us safe.
   Be with our waking,
   Be with our sleeping,
   Folding us round with
   Circles of love.

2 Mary, our mother,
  Working and planning,
  Making a home for
  Family and friends,
  Be with our working,
  Be with our resting,
  Keeping us active,
  Giving us sleep.

3 Mary, our mother,
  Hoping and longing,
  Planning a future
  That all can share,
  Be with our dreaming,
  Be with our longing,
  Filling our hearts with
  Castles of hope.

4 Mary, our mother,
  Leaping and dancing,
  Singing a song of
  Hoping fulfilled,
  Be with our laughing,
  Join in our feasting,
  Filling the earth with
  Patterns of joy.

Written in 1988, this was based on the experience of meditating on the statue of Mary at Fairacres Priory in the 1980s. Both 'Mary, our Mother' and 'Mary's Journey' (No. 37) have been used in services looking at the place of Mary in Christian devotion. The veneration of Mary proved for me an entry into the feminine in God, supported by Rosemary Radford Ruether's 'Mary: the Feminine Face of the Church' (SCM Presss, 1979) and Marina Warner's 'Alone of All Her Sex: Cult of the Virgin Mary' (latest edition Vintage, 2000). From Mary I moved to other areas of God's femininity, but it felt safer initially to be in an area that is well established in the church's devotion.

37 Mary's Journey

QUEM PASTORES 8.8.8.7.

German 14th-century carol
arranged June Boyce-Tillman (1943 –)

1 Mary, chosen to be mother
   Of a child in mystery hidden,
   Not o'ercome by fear or terror,
   Teach us how to persevere.

2 Mary, wandering through the desert,
   Travelling on uncertain, anxious,
   Held by arms, supporting, loving,
   Teach us how to persevere.

3 Mary, reaching Bethlehem's safety,
   Resting in a place so lowly,
   Giving birth in painful hoping,
   Teach us how to persevere.

4 Mary, dreaming of a future
   When her son would grow to manhood,
   Loving, trusting, planning, hoping,
   Teach us how to persevere.

I wrote this hymn in Perth, Australia, in August 1988. I did not find motherhood easy and this song using a tune associated with 'Jesus, good above all other' sees Mary as a model of perseverance as the original text does in Jesus.

38   A Wedding Blessing

1   May God's Wisdom deep within us (you)
Shape the joy within our (your) hearts,
Smooth the road we (you) travel gently,
Using all our (your) loving arts.

2   May fair blossoms dropping petals
On the living path we (you) tread,
Make a cushioned, glorious carpet,
Fragrancing the way ahead.

3   May we (you) root our (your) dreams and longings
In a true integrity,
Clearing out all that will hinder
Love's own creativity.

© Copyright 2006 Stainer & Bell Ltd

*This was written as a present for my son Matthew and his wife Andrea at their wedding in 1998.
The second person can be substituted for the first person throughout if desired, and any suitable
common-metre tune may be used, such as CROSS OF JESUS. The flower petals are used in
wedding ceremonies as a metaphor for a life of blessing. At my own wedding in 1972 we used Love
Maria Willis's 'Father, hear the prayer we offer', and there are echoes of this fine text in the images
here.*

Metre: CM

I prepared a version of this for the civil partnership of my friends David Page and Howard Norton:

1   May God's Wisdom deep within you
Shape the joy within your hearts,
Guide the route you share together,
Using all Her gentle arts.

2   May God clear the way before you,
Smooth the path with healing balm,
Shift the rubble, move the barriers,
Keep your love from all that harms.

3   May you root your dreams and longings
In a true integrity,
Clearing out all that will hinder
God's own creativity.

© Copyright 2006 Stainer & Bell Ltd

39 Music

1 Melody of God's grace, shape us,
   As we form life's curving phrase
   From the essence of your loving
   Flowing through each passing phase.
   May our lives reflect the singing
   Of the angels' endless praise.

2 Harmony of God's peace, move us
   To resolve disputes with love,
   So the discords drive us forward
   To the joy of heaven above.
   May our lives reflect the music
   Of the flying Spirit-dove.

3 Rhythm of God's order, structure
   Patterns of vitality.
   Vibrant pulse, your strength is flowing
   From hope's creativity.
   May our lives reflect your priesthood
   Dancing in humanity.

This was written for the tune PICARDY (see No. 27) in September 1998 for the ordination of my good friend the Rev. Professor Tony Kemp. His lifelong commitment to music education is reflected in the use of musical metaphors for the pattern of life. In the first verse we look at the melodic aspect of music, which is linear and links the present with the past and future. In the second verse we look at harmony, which is made up of chords. For about 500 years the pattern of Western harmony has been of a sense of moving forward – of movement rather than stasis – created by the need for discord to resolve to concord. Here in the metaphor we see the possibility of using apparently discordant times in our lives as springboards for understanding and new ways of living. The last verse celebrates the rhythmic aspect of music, linking its beat with the human pulse.

Metre: 8.7.8.7.8.7. Trochaic

40 Encompassing Love

1 O Christ, the holder of dark and light,
   Encircle me every day, each night.
   Our Lady, keeper of light and dark,
   Empower me within your strengthening love.

2 Stay close to me while I'm sleeping and
   While I'm standing and while I watch.
   Uphold me, embrace me gently,
   O source of encompassing loveliness.

3 O Mary, mother of Jesus child,
   Encircling arms around me fling!
   O Jesus, son of Mary maid,
   Fill me with the strength everlasting.

The words draw on Celtic sources which celebrate the complementarity of light and dark, and fit the tune GREENSLEEVES. The womb-shaped church of St Mary's Abbey, West Malling, which I visited regularly in the 1980s, with its openness to natural light, expresses the truths of encompassing love most clearly for me. Here Jesus and Mary are seen as interlinked theologically.

41 Pange Lingua Gloriosi

1 Of the body's glorious mystery
Make a song that all can sing.
Precious blood that flows so freely
Healing to the world can bring.
Joyfully the child of Mary
Is born for our empowering.

2 Given for us, given to us,
Through woman's integrity,
Jesus enters human discourse
Spreading words that set us free,
Dwelling with us, dwelling in us,
Ending his life wondrously.

3 On that last Passover evening,
Resting with his closest friends,
Carefully he marks the meaning
With the foods tradition sends,
His own self as food he's offering,
Giving it with his own hands.

4 God embodied makes a true bread
From his own humanity,
Makes a wine by pouring Christ-blood
Which our senses strain to see.
The sincere heart will be strengthened
Only with a faith set free.

5 So we kneel discerning Wisdom,
One with Christ in holiness;
And we give up ancient patterns,
Put new freedoms in their place,
Faith supporting human senses
By anxiety oppressed.

6 Praise creator, praise creation,
All the earth in glory sings.
Honour, strength and jubilation
Are the gifts that Wisdom brings.
All are joined in joy's elation,
For from God Creation springs.

Translated from the original Latin (possibly by Radegunda), this hymn was written in April 1998, at the request of the Rev. Jean Mayland, for a service in Durham Cathedral, which has a window dedicated to St Radegunda. It sees the Eucharist as a transformative ritual, an idea that has been very important in my thinking about this sacrament.

Metre: 8.7.8.7.8.7.

42   Count Me In

1 On a day when all were counted,
  Mary found no place to rest,
  Pressing forward with her burden,
  Sharing in our homelessness.

2 Jesus, born of exiled mother,
  Healer, friend of all the oppressed,
  Be with all who feel excluded,
  From the circles of the blessed.

3 You were also once at variance
  With the custom of your day,
  Breaking bonds of race and gender
  In your friends along the way.

4 Sister, brother, wife and mother –
  Could these all be names for you?
  Counsellor of ancient Wisdom,
  We would to ourselves be true.

This was written for a day course on inclusive language in worship run by the Wimbledon Liturgy Group and the Association for Inclusive Language in February 1990. The tune MARCHING fits these words, which relate to how the non-inclusive language of much traditional church worship amounts to the exclusion of women. Since 1990, thanks to the work of organisations such as the Association for Inclusive Language and Women in Theology, inclusive language has become increasingly accepted, certainly when referring to human beings. All my hymns use inclusive language, and, although the changing of traditional texts often causes angry reactions, most people like new texts using it. Ianthe Pratt has worked tirelessly in the Association for Inclusive Language to make available material in this area. She helped me finance my first published collections of material, 'In Praise of All-Encircling Love' I and II, and the collection of Hildegard translations 'Singing the Mystery'.

Metre: 8.7.8.7. Trochaic

43   Peace Dance

Form a circle, one behind the other. In line one step-close-step diagonally right (out of the circle) and then step-close-step diagonally left (into the circle). In line two face the centre and go into the middle, raising arms. In line three go out from the centre, lowering arms. In line four bring arms from feet to stretching (making a circle up high).

1   Peace flowing outward and peace flowing in,
    Draw peace from the centre in whom we begin;
    Find peace in the ending, the close of the day;
    Let peace in the heart wipe the evil away.

2   Strength flowing outward and strength flowing in,
    Draw strength from the centre in whom we begin;
    Find strength in the ending, the close of the day;
    Let strength in the heart wipe the evil away.

3   Hope flowing outward and hope flowing in,
    Draw hope from the centre in whom we begin;
    Find hope in the ending, the close of the day;
    Let hope in the heart wipe the evil away.

4   Joy flowing outward and joy flowing in,
    Draw joy from the centre in whom we begin;
    Find joy in the ending, the close of the day;
    Let joy in the heart wipe the evil away.

5   Love flowing outward and love flowing in,
    Draw love from the centre in whom we begin;
    Find love in the ending, the close of the day;
    Let love in the heart wipe the evil away.

On 31 August 1994 I set out on the blue boat to Rathlin Island off the beautiful North Antrim coast of Northern Ireland. I had just completed a course for teachers in Belfast and stayed with the Columbanus Community, dedicated to reconciliation. It was a splendid day and the small island (from which you can see both Scotland and Ireland) positively glowed. We went on a rickety minibus to the bird sanctuary at the far tip of the L-shaped island. It was here on a crackling transistor radio that I heard news of the IRA ceasefire. I walked back singing this text and finally sang it alone in the small Roman Catholic church where I lit a candle for the solution of Ireland's problems. It was first performed at a garden Eucharist in the home of my good friend, Ianthe Pratt, and should be sung to SLANE. The words echo 'Lord of all hopefulness', the text usually sung to this tune. 'Which' can be substituted for 'whom' in each verse if this is more acceptable to the group.

Metre: 10 11.11 11.

44 God the Strengthener

1 Praise to you, our great Creator,
   You rejoice when we are strong;
   Fill our hearts with loving power;
   Bring us wisdom with your song.
   Alleluia, alleluia,
   It's to you that we belong.

2 Praise to you, the Christ, Transformer,
   You have shared our wilderness;
   Lead us to the streams of mercy,
   Purify our bitterness.
   Alleluia, alleluia,
   Human God of gentleness.

3 Praise to you, the Holy Spirit,
   You can scorch us with your flame;
   Forge our love within your furnace,
   Burning guilt, destroying shame.
   Alleluia, alleluia,
   Dancing fire we cannot tame.

The ordination of women in the Church of England was a landmark for me. Many of my friends could now fulfil their vocation, and my hymn 'We shall go out with hope of resurrection' (No. 63), was widely used in this context. Several of my friends asked me to be present at their first Eucharist. Hilary Johnson, Chaplain at St George's Hospital (a colleague of my good friend Ian Ainsworth-Smith) asked me, but I was going to Hong Kong. This Trinitarian text was written for her and used on her first Eucharist in May 1994. It was also used by Clare Herbert in June of that year. The music is PRAISE MY SOUL. The opening line sees God rejoicing in our strength. There is a trope in hymnody summed up in 'We are but little children weak'. This has not worked well for women who wish to claim their authority, and strong women are regularly seen as overpowering or strident when in a man these qualities are associated with the prerogative to command. A critic wrote of the music of Ethel Smyth that it was strong music 'unbecoming from the pen of a woman'. There are still resonances of this thinking in the church.

Metre: 8.7.8.7.8.7. Trochaic

45 Hymn to Wisdom

1 Sing, dance and praise Wisdom in beautiful holiness;
   Love all-encircling in movement proclaim;
   Burn incense for worship, wear gold for her sovereignty,
   Bow low in reverence, Sophia's her name.

2 Courageously enter her courts in the mightiness
   Given to those who their truth bravely claim;
   For she will make circles of strength from their fearfulness,
   Dancing her comfort, for Mary's her name.

3 Now bend low before her and offload your carefulness;
   She'll purify it with transfiguring flame.
   In sheer foolish joy she will laugh away tearfulness,
   Dancing in suffering, for Christ is her name.

4 Tremendous and fascinating is the mystery
   Dancing in truth before creation's start;
   A strong vulnerability is Wisdom's paradox:
   Power and weakness entwined in God's heart.

This hymn was written on 1 January 1993, while I was staying with a Benedictine Community at St Mary's Abbey, West Malling, at a time of great crisis. It reflects Hildegard's thinking on Wisdom as well as my experience at the Abbey. This community, especially Sister Mary Paul and Sister Mary Gregory, who have affirmed my musical gifts, has been very significant in my spiritual journey. The hymn was first sung at one of the early liturgies of the organisation Catholic Women's Ordination, organised by Myra Poole SND, who has provided me with much affirmation. The tune is WAS LEBET, usually used for 'O worship the Lord in the beauty of holiness'. There are echoes of this text in such phrases as 'beautiful holiness', 'burn incense', 'wear gold'. Verse two celebrates people who will hold their truth in the face of fear. Verse three sees joy and sorrow closely intertwined and the use of 'foolish' reflects the Rev. Roly Bain's thinking on Christ, the Holy Fool (see No. 111) and Sydney Carter's 'Lord of the Dance'. Verse four looks at the central paradoxes of Christian theology.

Metre: 13.10.13.10.

46 Hymn for Times of Change

1 Sing high, sing low, swing free, let go,
   God of the turning round,
   In times of change may we discern
   The true angelic sound.
   For there are songs of gentler power,
   That warfare needs to hear.
   These nurturing sounds will bring us strength,
   And make the peace song clear.

2 Sing high, sing low, swing free, let go,
   God of the circling sphere,
   In looking back, may we discern
   The times you have been near.
   We face the joy, we touch the pain
   And give you thanks for both;
   We weave the two as glistening strands
   Within our travelling coat.

3 Sing high, sing low, swing free, let go,
   God of the open road,
   In moving on, may we discern
   The contents of our load;
   Help us to sift, help us to lose
   All we no longer need,
   That we may leap and dance and sing
   At your God-chosen speed.

Every New Year I go to stay at the Centre for Health and Pastoral Care at Holy Rood House, and we go to Ripon Cathedral to see the New Year in. I realised there were few hymns to celebrate this occasion, and wrote this text in January 1998, to be sung to the tune NOEL. This is usually used for the text 'It came upon the midnight clear' and the first verse has echoes of this and refers to the current media preoccupation with acts of violence rather than peace-making (see No. 77). In verse two it sees the need to integrate both joy and pain within our identity. Although written for the New Year, people have found this very useful for times of great change.

Metre: CMD

47 Spirit of Fire

IANTHE CM

June Boyce-Tillman (1943–)

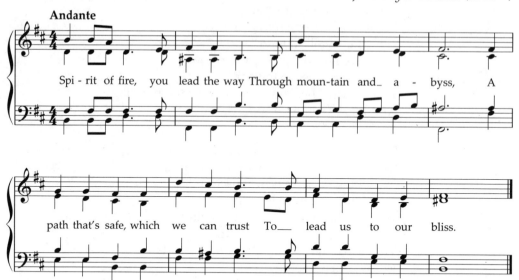

Spi - rit of fire, you lead the way Through moun-tain and_ a - byss, A path that's safe, which we can trust To_ lead us to our bliss.

2 Holy you are in giving life
To everything we know;
And, holy, too because your love
Through weeping wounds can flow.

3 Spirit of fire, infuse our hearts
With aromatic balm;
Anoint our lives with healing oil;
Preserve us from all harm.

4 Spirit of fire, you fit us well;
We need not be afraid;
As your firm garment gives support
For each one's tailor-made.

5 Spirit of fire, from you air flows,
And rivers lead their streams;
The character of burnished stones
Is hidden in your dreams.

6 Spirit of fire, you teach the wise
Your Wisdom to employ;
Their earnestness you purify;
They laugh within your joy.

7 Praise must be sung by all to you,
Who are their melody;
For you are life's symphonic song
That fills eternity.

This is a metrical version of Hildegard's 'O ignis spiritus'. The tune was first written for a set of words by William D. Horton and used in the Women in Theology publication 'Who are you looking for?' It formed the basis of a longer piece, performed by the King Alfred Singers in Poland. Its name acknowledges my debt to a long-standing friend, Ianthe Pratt, who first led me to Hildegard. The original hymn uses lively metaphors for the Holy Spirit, including in verse four the notion of a foundation garment, a concept very familiar to women of many generations. Verse three draws images from Hildegard's texts on healing. Aromatic balm could mean herbal tea.

48 Spirit of Justice

1 Spirit of Justice,
   Move in the world's heart,
   Making oases,
   Binding up wounds.
   In you the lame walk,
   Through you the blind see,
   With you the deaf talk,
   All is set free.

2 Spirit of Justice,
   Move in our own hearts.
   Bring us catharsis,
   Set us on fire.
   Let others' needing
   Temper our freedom;
   Shape all our hoping,
   Colour our dreams.

3 Spirit of Justice,
   We act within you:
   In your forgiveness.
   We claim your strength.
   Join in creation's
   Urge for completeness;
   Dance liberation's
   Powerful song.

This was written for a Eucharist on justice at Ianthe Pratt's house, and was sung to BUNESSAN (see No. 36). As a child I was brought up on the hymn book 'Songs of Praise'. The first overtly justice-centred hymn I met with was the text 'When through the whirl of wheels, and engines humming' as an adolescent.

Metre: 5.5.5.4.D.

49   Ocean Hymn

JENNY   6 6 5 6 6 5 7 8 6   June Boyce-Tillman (1943–)

Swell - ing, spark - ling oc - ean,__ Pulled_ by na - ture's
long - ing,__ Might-y ebb_ and_ flow.____ Mould us with_ your
surg - ing,__ Thrust_us__ in - to free - dom, Strength-en_ us_ with_
power. Depths_of cre - a - ti - vi - ty____ E - cho with_ a-
-bund - ant_ liv - ing, Pa - ra - digm of lov - ing.

1 Swelling, sparkling ocean,
  Pulled by nature's longing,
  Mighty ebb and flow.
  Mould us with your surging,
  Thrust us into freedom,
  Strengthen us with power.
  Depths of creativity
  Echo with abundant living,
  Paradigm of loving.

2 Diamond-studded blueness,
  Lace in foaming patterns
  Change, yet stay the same,
  Calm and sheltered harbours,
  Billowing, rolling breakers
  All form part of you.
  Deep within your sacred heart
  Seething with a love unending,
  Nature's joy delights us.

3 God within such beauty
  Pull us with your loving
  Into joyful deeps.
  Such majestic closeness
  Changing, yet unchanging
  Draws us to your heart.
  Gently sheltering harbour calm,
  Storms that wreck life's fragile fabric,
  All take place within you.

4 Keep us ever constant,
  Like your love that holds us
  Free yet ever joined.
  Ride the rolling breakers,
  Find in calmer waters
  Contrasts borne with joy.
  See within life's ebb and flow
  Patterns of your own creating,
  Rest within your changes.

This hymn was completed on the same day as Peace Dance (No. 43), on a hilltop overlooking the sparkling Atlantic, but had been planned long before. The American Hymn Society had a competition for a set of words to JESU MEINE FREUDE and I had trouble remembering the unusual metre of this tune (to which it may also be sung). I found it in the tiny Protestant church on Rathlin Island, copied it out and performed it alone, accompanying myself on the harmonium. The ideas and images, however, drew on my days spent exploring the Giant's Causeway and watching the Atlantic roll in on the North Antrim coast with my good friend Jenny Scharf in Coleraine, Northern Ireland, to whom it is dedicated.

50   A Celebration of Isaac Watts

1   The bells ring out, the bells ring in,
    God's praise is scattered wide;
    They bring God's overshadowing,
    A rolling, strengthening tide.

2   Ten thousand fill the streets below,
    A vibrant busy throng.
    Sufficient is God's hand alone
    Revealed in ancient song.

3   Our ancestors give us their hymns
    As wings of faith to rise
    Above the tangle of our sins
    And see with God's own eyes.

4   They turn our gaze towards the Cross,
    The axis of our world,
    That spreads God's loving like a robe
    Around the globe unfurled.

5   Christ's reign of peace is like the sun
    With circling golden ray.
    May here on earth God's will be done
    Within our lives today.

This hymn, which I wrote in September 1998, celebrates the fact that the bells of the Civic Centre clock in Southampton ring out the tune of ST ANNE every three hours. This is to celebrate Isaac Watts, whose hymn 'O God our help in ages past' is set to the tune ST ANNE, which is also the music for my text. I have included lines and ideas from five famous hymns by Watts: 'When I survey the wondrous cross'; 'Come, let us join our cheerful songs'; 'Give me the wings of faith to rise'; 'Jesus shall reign where'er the sun'; and 'O God, our help in ages past'. It formed the basis of a quiz in which people had to locate the lines within Watts's texts. I spent a great deal of my early life in Southampton and writing this hymn recalled hearing the chimes. I did not in the end manage to include 'There is a land of pure delight', which was written looking at Southampton from the Solent – a view I knew well and which incorporates the spire of St Mary's Church in whose choir I sang for fifteen years.

Metre: CM

51 Networking

1 The hope goes round,
   And the strength goes round,
   And the power goes round,
   And the love goes round;
   And hands are joined
   And our hearts are joined,
   And the Spirit is flowing between us.

   Wind circles that will encircle
   The earth, the sky and the deep abyss;
   Find loving entwined in networking,
   Claiming the strength that's our birthright.

2 For God, our God
   Is a hoping God,
   And a strengthening God,
   An empowering God;
   And God, our God
   Is a woven God,
   And the warp and the weft of creation.

   Dance joy in a cosmic circle
   A toughened strand in the cloth of God;
   Weave shapes of a true integrity;
   This is the stuff of creation.

'Networking' was written at the request of the Catholic Women's Network for their Tenth Jubilee in June 1994. It was first sung in Ripon Cathedral to GREENSLEEVES, and used for dance. It is best to use the first seven lines only, repeated, for dancing. There was a huge growth in networks of all kinds in the late-twentieth century culminating in the development of the internet. A theology of interconnectedness developed alongside this, especially in the writing of Professor Mary Grey.

52 Embracing the Darkness

1 The winter sun is hanging low
And bare outlines are clear;
But trees and sky and distant shore,
All merge as night draws near.
For deepening dark makes all things one,
Life's mystery appears;
A secret time, a dreaming place
Bring God's touch to our fears.

2 We chart our paths by careful lights,
Make sure our way is safe;
But intuition also guides,
The shaded way of faith.
Chorus

3 We seek our truth by reasoned steps,
So we are sure we know;
But when we don't, we can be calm
And let the struggling go.
Chorus

4 With rigid rules we can feel safe,
For structures hold us tight:
But leaping faith, embracing play,
Conceives a child at night.
Chorus

This was written for a meeting of the Southampton Creation Spirituality Group led by my good friend, Professor Chris Clarke, for Advent 1994. The tune is KINGSFOLD. It was written on the Hog's Back near Guildford. The winter sun was low and the trees did look very clear. Like No. 31 it celebrates darkness, here as a unifying force. It sets out the need for balance as in No. 24. I was then just entering the research culture at King Alfred's College, Winchester and verses two, three and four reflect a need to balance all the careful planning that characterises that culture with the intuitive leap of faith in the creative process. The hymn refers to God touching us. I have learned through the use of therapeutic massage the power of touch in healing with people like my good friends Pat Macey and Helen Arundel, who have soothed away many hurts.

Metre: CMD

53   Eucharist

IAN SM   June Boyce-Tillman (1943–)

1 The wounds are human wounds;
  The tears are human tears;
  Two loving friends beside a cross
  Pour love in spite of fears.

2 In broken human form
  That Christ still lives today,
  And human love can still be poured
  To wipe the pain away.

3 The loving joy of God
  Is poured out in our wine;
  The bread reveals our brokenness,
  Christ's body in the vine.

4 In sharing grief and pain
  And joyful, laughing love,
  We are a priesthood here on earth
  Reflecting God above.

Written on 17 September 1992, St Hildegard's Day, for the twenty-fifth anniversary of the ordination of the Rev. Canon Ian Ainsworth-Smith, Chaplain of St George's Hospital, Tooting. It reflects themes from his life – the Eucharist, support of women's ordination and empathy with the suffering. I was admitted to St George's with acute depression in the 1970s and, working through faith, Ian enabled me to manage my depressive temperament by means of creativity. The Rev. Janet Wootton, a great colleague in hymn writing, helped shape verse three. On the day after ending anti-depressants following a family birth and death it was as if the flood tide of hymnody was released.

54 New Life

NEW LIFE   8.7.8.7. trochaic and Chorus

June Boyce-Tillman (1943–)

There is dark-ness in the night-time When the world is fast a-sleep;— But the sun breaks through at morn-ing Af-ter soft re-fresh-ing sleep. Sing Ho--san-na, al-le-lu-ya, Out of dark-ness comes the light.

Optional instruments

2 There is darkness in the garden
   When the seeds are buried deep;
   But in the springtime comes awakening
   New life leaps from winter sleep.
   Chorus

3 There was darkness in the city
   When the bombers thudded in;
   But a time came for rebuilding
   And for peace to reconcile.
   Chorus

4   There is darkness in our living
    When the world seems parched and dry
    But deep down are springs of healing
    Welling up in time of need.
    Chorus

5   There was darkness in the money
    Which betrayed the trust of friends,
    But the evening brought the laughter
    Of the food and drink that's shared.
    Chorus

7   There was darkness in the courtroom
    When the crowd yelled out for blood,
    But the struggle up the hillside
    Brought a stranger's helping hand.
    Chorus

6   There was darkness in the greeting
    When his friends all ran away,
    There was still a time for healing
    And for hate turned into love.
    Chorus

8   There was darkness on the hillside
    When they killed the rebel king;
    But the evening brought a resting,
    Winding sheets in tomb of stone.
    Chorus

9   There was darkness in the garden
    And the world seemed hushed in awe
    When the gravestone cracked right open
    And the tomb gave up its power.
    Chorus

10 There was darkness in the weeping
    When they all thought he was dead;
    But the morning brought the gladness
    Of reunion with a friend.
    Chorus

11 Out of night-time comes the sunrise:
    Out of winter comes the spring;
    Out of death there comes a rising,
    God has sent us his own Spring.
    Chorus

This was the first hymn I ever wrote, for a local hymn competition in 1978. I did not win and it was another eight years before I wrote another one! It was in many ways a prototype for No. 31 which is a more sophisticated treatment of a theme that runs through my work. I have been concerned about the concentration of light in Christianity especially in the Johannine texts. This has skewed our view of difficult times in our lives and has been projected on black-skinned ethnic groups in a very unhelpful way.

55 St Brigid Hymn

1 There is a warmth within each heart
   That's called the sacred fire.
   God breathes and fans it into life;
   The flames of love rise higher.

2 The gates of generosity
   Swing wide within our hearts;
   We build communities of love
   Where loneliness departs.

3 With praise we tend that holy flame
   As Brigid did before.
   In prayer, God, consecrate our lives
   And make our roots secure.

Extra verses for the taking of vows:

4 Brigid, come, accept the vow
   That each member offers now,
   With your strength their life endow,
   Holy Spirit, fill them.

5 Now on this community,
   Pour thy power and charity,
   Strengthen its integrity,
   Holy Spirit, fill us.

This was written in April 2002, to the tune HOUSE OF THE RISING SUN, for my friend, the Rt Rev. Professor Elizabeth Stuart, to celebrate the founding of the Order of St Brigid. I thought the choice of music – a tune associated with a house of street women – was an interesting play on St Brigid's hospitality. St Brigid's Community kept the sacred fire continually burning in Celtic Ireland. We need in prayer to tend this flame in our own hearts.

Metre: CM

56   A Carol for Christmas Night

1   This is the long night of white drifting snow,
    White snow that will be there till it is day,
    White moon that will be there till it is morn,
    And the bells of paradise, I heard them ring.

2   Eve of nativity, great mystery,
    Eve of the birth of the virgin's own son,
    Jesus is born on this glorious night,
    And I love my Lord Jesus above anything.

3   Ere it was heard that the glory had come,
    Ere it was heard that his foot had reached earth,
    Heard was the wave breaking full on the shore,
    And the bells of paradise, I heard them ring.

4   Born on this night is the root of our joy,
    Gleaming this night is the sun o'er the hills;
    Gleaming this night are the shore and the sea,
    And I love my Lord Jesus above anything.

5   Ere came the news that the pain had been borne,
    Ere came the message that born was her child,
    Heard was the song of the angels of peace.
    And the bells of paradise, I heard them ring.

*I set these words, based on a Celtic source, to a favourite English carol tune, 'Down in yon forest'.
It was first sung as an introit to the midnight mass in the chapel of St George's Hospital, Tooting,
in 1989, where I have played for the midnight Christmas Eucharist for twenty years. The last
lines of each verse are taken from 'Down in yon forest'. It contains a great sense of mystery in the
paradoxes it presents in the sun gleaming at night. The original text of the tune, with its curious
reference to a bleeding knight, sometimes linked with Corpus Christi, is similarly mysterious in
origin and meaning.*

Metre: 10.10.10.11. Irregular

57   The Year of Jubilee

1 This is the Year of Jubilee,
   Weep for the world and set it free.
   Sing for a shared community.
   Alleluia, alleluia, alleluia.

2 This is the Year of Jubilee,
   Bind up the wounds, set people free,
   Sing for a shared community.
   Alleluia, alleluia, alleluia.

3 This is the Year of Jubilee,
   Cancel the debts, set people free,
   Sing for a shared community.
   Alleluia, alleluia, alleluia.

4 This is the Year of Jubilee,
   Strengthen the weak and set them free,
   Sing for a shared community.
   Alleluia, alleluia, alleluia.

5 This is the Year of Jubilee,
   Transform the strong and set them free,
   Sing for a shared community.
   Alleluia, alleluia, alleluia.

6 This is the Year of Jubilee,
   Dance in the world and set it free,
   Sing for a shared community.
   Alleluia, alleluia, alleluia.

This is a song, at present based on liberation theology, of simple structure and to be sung to GELOBT SEI GOTT (see No. 21).It is designed to be adapted for particular occasions. The pattern is one of three unchanging lines and one that can be changed. Here are some other possible adaptations:

(a) A hymn linked to Luke Chapter 4 could include as third lines for each verse:
   Help the lame walk and set them free
   Make the blind see and set them free
   Help the dumb speak and set them free

(b) A hymn on an ecological theme could include as third lines for each verse:
   Strengthen the trees and set them free
   Care for the earth and set it free

These are a few of the possibilities. The song could also be used to summarise a group discussion by including resolutions as lines or with spontaneous improvisation by individuals or groups.

Metre: 8 8 8.12.

58 Funeral Hymn

1 We bring our gratitude to you
   For guidance in our lives,
   For those whose love has touched our hearts
   And made our souls revive.

2 We bring our thanks for caring strength
   That holds us on our way,
   And brings us closer to your heart,
   And drives our fear away.

3 For human hands can foster hope
   And make our pathway clear,
   Support us in our weaknesses
   And make your love come near.

4 We ask your blessing for these souls
   As on through death they speed,
   And pray that you will bless us too
   With all the strength we need.

5 Our hearts are filled with healing love
   And overflowing grace.
   Our roots are formed by faith in you;
   We feel your warm embrace.

This hymn was writen for the funeral of my ex-father-in-law William (Bill) Tillman, whose friendship I had valued greatly and who, in his dying, had allowed me to gain greater understanding of what this involves. I was allowed to wash and dress his body after his death, which was a deeply moving experience. I had watched by his bedside while he was unconscious and dying, and sung hymns into his ear. I had anointed him with rose oil which I also used on the dead body. The experience enabled me to understand dying as a process rather than a single moment. I sang this hymn at a memorial service for my good friend, Oliver Pratt, and read it at Bill's funeral. The fifth verse was added in 2006 in memory of the wife of Ronald van Cooten, of St Paul's, Furzedown, the London church where I have worshipped for the last thirty years. ST ANNE is a suitable tune.

Metre: CM

59   Ecumenical Hymn

For Robert Kaggwa

1   We gather here together
From different ways of faith.
Your mystery calls us forward
Into the heart of grace.
We know your truth is wider
Than all we can expect;
So here we seek communion
In love and with respect.

2   We own our faith in Jesus
Who made your essence known;
And hope we have been faithful
To what we have been shown.
We share our partial insights
And find you are our rest.
And so become empowered
With love and with respect.

3   Your spirit flows between us
And makes your being clear.
Diversely reuniting
We sense your presence here;
And so your church can mirror
The world you resurrect,
As gently we draw nearer
In love and in respect.

Written 30 January 2006, it is to be sung to the tune THORNBURY. I have worked with the Rev. Dr Robert Kaggwa in Eucharists at Ianthe Pratt's house for many years. He has supported my vocation to the priesthood and has given me his beautiful stole in which to be ordained. I feel very honoured that I shall be wearing a gift from a Roman Catholic priest from Uganda. I wrote this text for an ecumenical service at Digby Stuart College, Roehampton University, where he is chaplain, on 26 February 2006. The tune is usually associated with 'Your hand, O God, has guided', with the recurring refrain 'one church, one faith, one Lord'. This text suggests that unity is based on respect for difference not uniformity, and that there will always be a diversity of beliefs and practices within the church.

Metre: 7.6.7.6.D.

60 Hymn for 100 Years of Women's Ordination

We rejoice, we rejoice in our foremothers' faith;
We rejoice, we rejoice in an inclusive grace;
We'll keep pressing onwards in courage and love
And soar on the wings of God's free-flowing dove.

1 God groans as she watches us struggle and fight;
   Her belly is stretching and aching for right;
   Tears flow in her travail; her pain is revealed;
   She waits and she hopes that her wounds may be healed.
   Chorus

2 God's wings are enfolding and circling the earth;
   She dreams of the time when she brought it to birth,
   Laments how the systems of patriarchs' power
   Have stopped her from bringing her world into flower.
   Chorus

3 God bristles with anger and rage in her bones;
   Her body is raped and emitting deep moans;
   Her energy rises; she raises her arm
   To regain the power for all who are harmed.
   Chorus

4 God joys in our leaping our dances of faith;
   She laughs as she opens her arms in embrace;
   We gather within her as sisters in grace;
   Our strength is increasing as we find our place.
   Chorus

This hymn was written in June 2004 for a service in the American Episcopal Church in Tottenham Court Road to celebrate 100 years of women's ordination by the Society for Women's Ministry. For the music I chose TO GOD BE THE GLORY, a tune associated with the famous hymn 'To God be the glory' by Fanny Crosby (Frances Jane van Alstyne (1820–1915)). This strong tune evokes the spirit of the suffragettes, recalling Gertrude von Petzold, the first Unitarian minister. It had that feel when sung at the Britain and Ireland School of Feminist Theology at Bristol University in 2004 and women took their scarves and waved them, swaying like a football crowd. Originally there was a fear that this strong tune would not find acceptance in feminist circles taken up with the vulnerability of God. It is so difficult for women to claim their strength (see No. 44). This was my first hymn to use 'she' confidently for God.

Metre: 11 11.11 11. and Chorus 12 12.11 11.

61 Wedding Hymn

1 We set out in our search for truth
   And scan the soaring heavens.
   We plumb the ancient ocean's depths
   And search the deepening caverns.
   The elders yield their secrets up,
   In anecdote and story,
   While dark-robed nuns the office sing
   In praise of God's great glory.

2 Yet there's a find to every search
   Some rest for every traveller.
   In foolish joy the dancing God
   Can meet us at a corner.
   Our longing love then reaches out
   And finds an answering echo.
   We sense a prayerful soul's response,
   A healing for our shadow.

3 The joining of two loving hearts
   Brings all of us together;
   And helps us in the circle dance
   Enfolding earth for ever.
   A new found couple joins the ring;
   The eternal band is swinging.
   We catch the song of endless love
   And ask to join the singing.

This text was specially written for and first sung at the wedding of Dr Angie Cotter and Neil Leary in December 1992 at the Church of Holy Trinity, Rotherhithe. It draws on the experience of these two good friends but could be used for any 'seekers of the truth'. It includes references to many aspects of their life such as care for the elderly and the nuns of Malling Abbey. The tune is GOLDEN SHEAVES.

Metre: 8.7.8.7.D.

62   Commitment to Creation

1   We shall go out renewed in our commitment
    To integrate creation in ourselves,
    To work and trust, to hope and play and wonder
    With hearts that long for world integrity.
    We'll work to right the wrongs of devastation
    Of humankind and all created life;
    We'll dream our dreams of earth's reintegration
    Within the dreamtime of a Christ who is the Way.

2   We'll play our games that still the hectic struggle
    To win a race that all can only lose;
    We'll trust the God who works from deep within us
    For peace and justice, unity for all.
    We'll keep alive the flame of hope within us
    And wonder still at beauty yet unborn.
    We'll leap and dance the resurrection story,
    Including all within the circles of our love.

This was written in February 1995 for Matthew Fox's visit to Southampton (at the request of Professor Chris Clarke). He is a leading figure in the development of creation spirituality (ecotheology) – hence, line two indicating our need to feel ourselves part of the natural world. He also critiques the competitiveness of contemporary culture as in verse two, line two. Chris Clarke leads Greenspirit, which disseminates ecotheological ideas. He and Isabel have encouraged the use of my material in these circles as I often use the natural world in my hymns. This text was inspired by a visit to Canberra in 1995 and the hospitality of Lyndsay and Sylvia Cleland who introduced me to Australian-style creation spirituality. It should be sung to LONDONDERRY (see No. 63).

Metre: 11.10.11.10.11.10.11.12.

63   Resurrection Hope

LONDONDERRY   11.10.11.10.11.10.11.12.

Traditional Irish
arranged June Boyce-Tillman (1943–)

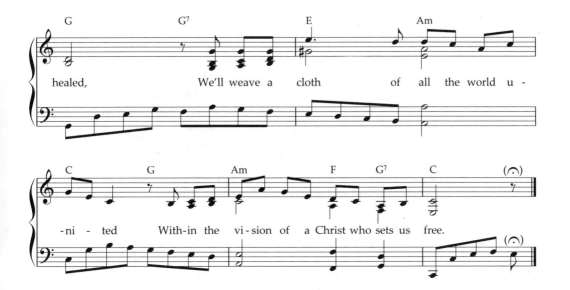

healed, We'll weave a cloth of all the world u-
-ni - ted With-in the vi-sion of a Christ who sets us free.

1 We shall go out with hope of resurrection,
   We shall go out, from strength to strength go on,
   We shall go out and tell our stories boldly,
   Tales of a love that will not let us go.
   We'll sing our songs of wrongs that can be righted,
   We'll dream our dream of hurts that can be healed,
   We'll weave a cloth of all the world united
   Within the vision of a Christ who sets us free.

2 We'll give a voice to those who have not spoken,
   We'll find the words for those whose lips are sealed,
   We'll make the tunes for those who sing no longer,
   Vibrating love alive in every heart.
   We'll share our joy with those who are still weeping,
   Chant hymns of strength for hearts that break in grief,
   We'll leap and dance the resurrection story
   Including all within the circles of our love.

My hymn 'We shall go out with hope of resurrection' was composed in 1992 for a liturgy in Southwark Cathedral written by Nicola Slee for the Southwark Ordination Course entitled 'Broken Silence – Women Finding a Voice', which also included a motet incorporating women screaming. It has been used for a wide variety of situations, including weddings, funerals and a service on World AIDS Day in Westminster Abbey. If any hymn outlives me, I think it will be this one! I have many personal memories of the use of this hymn. One is its use at the inauguration of Archbishop Sentamu (who also chose this hymn for his inaugural service as Bishop of Birmingham). Another very different one is of my good friend Mary O'Reagan singing the first verse as a solo by the fountain in the chapel at Liverpool Hope University as part of a liturgy at a Britain and Ireland School of Feminist Theology conference.

64 Graduation Hymn

1 We shall go out with gratitude within us
   For signposts, guides and waymarks in our lives,
   And friendships formed in laughter and in sadness;
   For when we sense support, our hearts revive.
   May we in strength fulfil the needs of others,
   Not let our fear destroy the truth within;
   May we seek justice for a whole creation
   (And stay) in tune with one who is our origin.

2 We praise this source of all that is created,
   The model of our creativity;
   May we be one with all that is life-giving,
   Not lose our way in negativity.
   For we would walk in happiness and sorrow,
   Yet keep in touch with wellsprings deep inside;
   So shall we come to know abundant living,
   And share in God a love (that is) both deep and wide.

In an attempt to provide a text that can be sung conscientiously by a group of students of different beliefs, I wrote this hymn for the 1993 graduation ceremony at King Alfred's College of Higher Education, Winchester. The words can be sung either to LONDONDERRY (see No. 63) or to INTERCESSOR (if the latter, with the bracketed material omitted).

Metre: 11.10.11.10.11.10.11.12. or 11.10.11.10.D.

65 Love

1 We sing a love that sets all people free,
   That blows like wind, that burns like scorching flame,
   Enfolds like earth, springs up like water clear.
   Come, living love, live in our hearts today.

2 We sing a love that seeks another's good,
   That longs to serve and not to count the cost,
   A love that, yielding, finds itself made new.
   Come, caring love, live in our hearts today.

3 We sing a love, unflinching, unafraid
   To be itself, despite another's wrath,
   A love that stands alone and undismayed.
   Come, strengthening love, live in our hearts today.

4 We sing a love that, wandering, will not rest
   Until it finds its way, its home, its source,
   Through joy and sadness pressing on refreshed.
   Come, pilgrim love, live in our hearts today.

5 We sing a burning, fiery, Holy Ghost
   That seeks out shades of ancient bitterness,
   Transfiguring these, as Christ in every heart.
   Come joyful love, live in our hearts today.

This text was commissioned in March 1988 as a 'politically right' wedding hymn. Drawing on personal experience, I combined metaphors from the natural world with notions of two other loves: the self-giving yielding love, and the love that stands firm 'despite another's wrath'. The last verse reflects the fact that many marriages fail because of elements in our background of which we are no longer conscious. 'Holy Ghost' is used here deliberately to counteract the 'shades of bitterness'. Though this use of a possible archaism has been questioned, sometimes an older word can be reclaimed now with a power lacking in more familiar words. It is sung to the tune WOODLANDS and has been used in many different contexts by groups of people who feel they are oppressed.

Metre: 10.10.10.10.

66   The Wise People

WE THREE KINGS OF ORIENT

J. H. Hopkins (1820–1891)
arranged June Boyce-Tillman (1943–)

We, the wise, from O-ri-ent are; Bear-ing gifts, we tra-verse a-far;

Field and foun-tain, moor and moun-tain, Fol-low-ing yon-der star. O,___

star of won-der, star of light, Star of roy-al beau-ty bright,

West-ward lead-ing, still pro-ceed-ing, Guide us to thy per-fect light.

1 We, the wise, from Orient are;
   Bearing gifts, we traverse afar;
   Field and fountain, moor and mountain,
   Following yonder star.
   O, star of wonder, star of light,
   Star of royal beauty bright,
   Westward leading, still proceeding,
   Guide us to thy perfect light.

Caspar
(a tailor)

2 Gold gives clothes a beauty so rare,
   Sarees, shawls and copes we can wear,
   Make our bodies shine with the radiance of
   God-given temples fair.
   Chorus

Melchior
(an aromatherapist)

3 Frankincense we burn in a shrine;
   Perfumes tell us we are divine;
   Lotions, oils, all aromas
   The God within bring to mind.
   Chorus

Balthazar
(a masseur)

4 Myrrh in massage tells us we're loved,
   Helps to soothe the place that is rough,
   Makes us feel a warm acceptance
   On earth as in heaven above.
   Chorus

5 Glorious now we all can arise,
   Parts of God's own sacrifice.
   Heaven sings alleluia,
   Alleluia the earth replies.
   Chorus

This hymn was written at the request of Professor Mary Grey, from whom I have learned so much,
for an Epiphany liturgy at the Retreat Association annual conference in January 1991. Adapted
from the famous original by J. H. Hopkins, the text reflects my interest in forms of natural healing.

67 The Weaver

1 Weave, weave, weave the winding cloth
   Of colours from the world;
   Shoot, shoot, shoot the shuttle through
   And let the form unfurl.
   The dark thread is for grieving;
   Love's search can cause us pain;
   But brighter strands are mingling,
   Restoring hope again.

2 Pull, pull, pull the weft pick tight
   To integrate the weave;
   Blend, blend, blend the separate threads,
   A unity achieve.
   Come weave our hearts together
   With yarn of sparkling hues;
   And make convincing patterns
   As all our colours fuse.

3 Weave, weave, weave a sturdy cloth;
   Your love will make it strong;
   Sing, sing, sing, you angel choirs
   And strengthen it with song.

Written in June 1993, this hymn owes a great deal to my friendship with Richard Hopper and Evelyn Ross (a weaver), who were important members of the liturgy group that strengthened me a great deal through its gatherings in Wimbledon. The tune is ROYAL OAK, which is used as an eight-line tune with no chorus. The last verse uses just the chorus tune. The chosen image is of God as weaver, seeing the task of redeeming as being one of enabling the grieving and joy to be woven together. This draws on images of three women weaving the world, as in the Norns of Norse mythology.

Metre: 7.6.7.6.D.

68   Who are These Outside the Barred Gates?

For Carol

1   Who are these outside the barred gates
    Looking in with woeful stare?
    These are those who share Christ's exile
    While our world stays unaware.
    May we see the Christ inside
    So that God is not denied.

2   Who are these with hands extended,
    Bellies stretched and cups unfilled?
    These are those who share Christ's hunger
    Showing God can still be killed.
    Chorus

3   Who are these abused and bruised by
    Those responsible for care?
    These are they who share Christ's passion
    In a world deeply unfair.
    Chorus

4   Who are these ensnared and fettered,
    Freedom gone and worth denied?
    These are those who share Christ's prison
    And the death that he defied.
    Chorus

5   Who are these entrapped, addicted
    To a substance that can harm?
    These are they who share Christ's longing
    For a place of bliss and calm.
    Chorus

This was written on 28 October 2005, to be sung to the tune ALL SAINTS (Darmstadt). I was preaching at St Paul's, Furzedown on the theme of the parable of the sheep and the goats, which is a favourite of mine. I chose the theme of the Christ in everyone, especially those who are marginalised. The last verse reflects conversations concerning drug addiction and the motivation of addicts which I had with my long-standing friend, Lorna Nunn, with whom I have sung in the choir of St Paul's, Furzedown for twenty-five years. Carol Boulter affirmed this text, which I sang to her over the phone, and so it is dedicated to her.

Metre: 8.7.8.7. and Chorus 7 7.

69 Hymn for Justice

HUGH'S BREASTPLATE

June Boyce-Tillman (1943–)

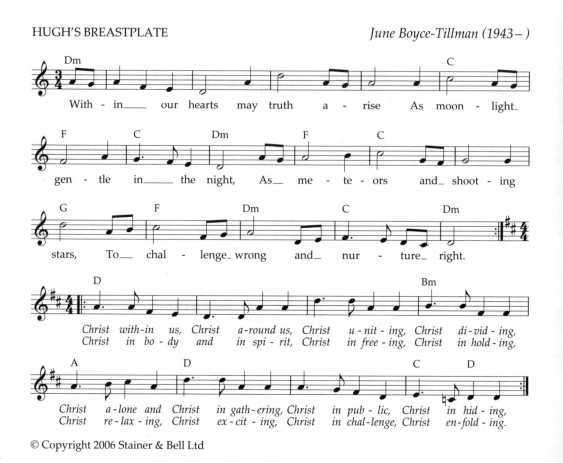

With - in___ our hearts may truth a - rise As moon - light_
gen - tle in___ the night, As_ me - te - ors and_ shoot - ing
stars, To_ chal - lenge_ wrong and_ nur - ture_ right.

Christ with-in us, Christ a-round us, Christ u - nit - ing, Christ di - vid - ing,
Christ in bo - dy and in spi - rit, Christ in free - ing, Christ in hold - ing,

Christ a - lone and Christ in gath-ering, Christ in pub - lic, Christ in hid - ing,
Christ re - lax - ing, Christ ex - cit - ing, Christ in chal-lenge, Christ en-fold - ing.

For Hugh Boulter

1 Within our hearts may truth arise
   As moonlight gentle in the night,
   As meteors and shooting stars,
   To challenge wrong and nurture right.

2 Within our hearts may wisdom grow,
   Like rhizomes spreading in the earth,
   Conjoining different faith insights
   To bring new paradigms to birth.

3 Within our hearts may peace prevail,
   And ripple like a bubbling spring,
   To bring earth's deserts into bloom,
   So from the margins joy can ring.

4 Within our hearts may justice reign
   And burn with fiery Spirit-flames,
   Creating systems that in strength
   Embody Christ's outrageous claims.

   Christ within us, Christ around us,
   Christ uniting, Christ dividing,
   Christ alone and Christ in gathering,
   Christ in public, Christ in hiding,
   Christ in body and in spirit,
   Christ in freeing, Christ in holding,
   Christ relaxing, Christ exciting,
   Christ in challenge, Christ enfolding.

5 And so the God of joy and hope,
   Can be revealed in humankind,
   Where politics reflect shared wealth
   And nature's growth as intertwined.

I wrote this hymn on a sunny day in August 1999 in the garden of Carol and Hugh Boulter, as a present for Hugh's birthday in January 2000, and commissioned by Carol, who has been immensely supportive of my work. The text has a breastplate structure built of themes from Hugh's life, for example, education, the project 'Wells for India', and his interfaith work. The breastplate with which we are most familiar through the one entitled St Patrick's breastplate was essentially a spiritual shield or strengthener that each person constructs from objects and ideas that they find strengthening, not unlike the medicine shields and wheels of the North American Indian tradition. The tune ST PATRICK can also be used. It was first sung in the chapel of Prasada at Montauroux in France, the house of Cecile and Jean CGA, where Pam Gladding and I have gained such refreshment. It is recorded on the CD 'Voice of Experience' which was commissioned by Carol for Hugh. The image of the rhizome in verse two uses the structure of the roots of plants like irises where under the earth there are tubes with nodal points spreading gradually. The postmodern philosopher, Deleuze, uses this image for the way we grow by being nomadic and developing meandering structures based on the variety of our experiences.

70   Wisdom Hymn

1   Wisdom will set us free!
     Work for community;
     Value diversity
     Held in a unity.
     Act justly with respect today!
     We hear God's call and we obey.

2   Wisdom will set us free!
     Weep with the damaged earth;
     Losing fertility,
     Longing to find rebirth.
     Show mercy to the world today!
     We hear God's call and we obey.

3   Wisdom will set us free!
     Walk with the silent poor;
     Share with humility;
     Open the freedom door.
     Come, prophets, shout your words today!
     We hear God's call and we obey.

4   Wisdom will set us free!
     Leap with the angel clown
     Dancing vitality
     Through city, hamlet, town.
     Rejoice creatively today!
     We hear God's call and we obey.

5   Wisdom will set us free!
     Make the thanksgiving song;
     Echo the praise of heaven
     To which we all belong.
     Rework the Wisdom theme today!
     We hear God's call and we obey.

Set to LITTLE CORNARD, this is an adaptation of a hymn commissioned by Churches Together in Britain and Ireland for the Queen's Golden Jubilee. It originally included a verse celebrating her working out of her own vocation. It was included in my cantata 'The Healing of the Earth', which was sung by 300 children in Battersea Technology College, London. It is intended to be appropriate for a multi-faith society. The clown figure in verse four may be identified with Jesus (see No. 111). The image recalls figures like Will Kempe, the morris dancer who danced from one end of England to the other in the reign of Elizabeth I. The hymn is based on Micah 6. Verse one deals with acting justly, verse two with loving mercy for the earth, and verse three with walking with the humble poor and with prophets like Donald Soper who spoke for them at Speakers' Corner. The final verse sees how each age must rework the Wisdom call in its own way.

Metre: 6.6.6.6.8 8.

71 Thanksgiving for the Birth of a Baby

1 Womanly Wisdom
  Seeking the form of God,
  Uttered a prayer
  From the depth of a heart:
  'Give me a baby,
  Body of loveliness,
  Crown for my heart, my soul's delight.'

2 Infinite Wisdom
  Granted a saintly prayer.
  This was her song
  As she nursed her own son:
  'My child is beauty,
  My child is loveliness,
  He is my soul's delight and crown.'

3 'My little baby
  Gives me a greater wealth
  Than all the princes
  And priests of the earth.
  In him is Jesus,
  Lord of all loveliness.
  He is my soul's delight and crown.'

4 'My little Jesus,
  Noble, angelic one,
  Not born a priest
  But a Jewess's son.
  Jesus is beauty,
  Jesus is loveliness,
  He is my soul's delight and crown.'

5 Little Lord Jesus,
  Tiny, yet powerful,
  If you will pray
  To him he will forgive.
  Jesus is beauty,
  Jesus is loveliness,
  He is my soul's delight and crown.

6 O my Lord Jesus,
  My everlasting good,
  Freely you give
  And nothing withhold.
  You are all beauty;
  You are all loveliness;
  You are my soul's delight and crown.

Set to the tune SCHÖNSTER HERR JESU (also known as ASCALON), this hymn, written in August 1988, is based on the story of St Ide. She said she would believe if God gave her a baby. She bore a child and became a holy woman. It also reflects what I have learned from my own experience of motherhood and how the story of Mary and Jesus helped me. It was first sung at St Paul's Church, Tooting, in a concert entitled 'Sound of Women's Silence'.

Metre: 5.6.4.6.5.6.8.

72 A Hymn for the Women's Synod

1 You have called us here together
   Bringing gifts from different parts,
   Sharing stories, love and worship,
   Linking arms and joining hearts.

2 Shamrock shows your many facets;
   Daffodil shouts 'Life made new!'
   Rose has sharpness in its loving;
   Thistle blends with heaven's blue.

3 We are flowers in your garden;
   Each reveals a new insight;
   Rippling streams and fragrant blossoms
   Dance in resurrection light.

4 We are nurtured in your garden;
   Fountains play and wounds are healed;
   May we draw on earth's deep sweetness
   So your love can be revealed.

This was written in April 1999, for the Women's Synod of Wales, Ireland, Scotland and England (WISE) in Liverpool. Although flowers represented the various countries, some were uncomfortable with their being used as a metaphor for women, which was seen as representing an outmoded model of femininity. Any upbeat 8.7.8.7. trochaic tune would be appropriate, for example HALTON HOLGATE or CASTIGLIONE.

Metre: 8.7.8.7. Trochaic

73 A Hymn for King Alfred's Day

1 Your supporting presence guides us through the night
   So we can approach you, sparkling source of light;
   Shine through the mists, the deadening heavy clay.
   Purifying Spirit, burn the dross away.

2 You are gentler weather after winter's rains,
   And a wayside restplace soothing journeying's strains;
   Though out in front, protect us with yourself,
   You're our destination and the road itself.

A request from Professor John Dickinson, Principal of King Alfred's College of Higher Education, Winchester, to link with St Bartholomew's Church, Hyde (where King Alfred's grave lies) prompted this paraphrase of his translation of Boethius. It was written on a plane taking me on my first visit to the USA in July 1994, and was first used on 26 October (King Alfred's Day) in college and at St Bartholomew's. The tune is NOËL NOUVELET.

Metre: 11 11.10 11.

Songs

My songs belong to a more personal world than my hymns, where the demands of public expression are less in conflict with intimacy, the tradition of oracy, and the possibilities of spontaneous expression. The personal note extends to aspects of my own journey, as in *Flesh of one flesh*, written for my mother, or songs written for particular occasions such as *Lullaby*, composed for a healing service to remember an abortion of many years before. As with my hymns, locality has been a vital stimulus to creativity in my song writing, and the circumstances under which many of them came into being, often simply as 'given' things that arrived, are explained in the notes.

These songs are intended to be sung in unison, and my own preference is to accompany them with a drum or guitar, or with both if available. In such simple structures it is very easy to make new verses as the context demands, and it should be possible to do so without notated music or words. Sometimes I sing the verses and people join in the chorus by ear, which can be useful when the singers must also clap or participate in some other way as well as singing, as in the clown song *Put on your patchwork trousers*. And again, a return to oracy in the church's traditions is important here.

74 A-Godding

June Boyce-Tillman (1943–)

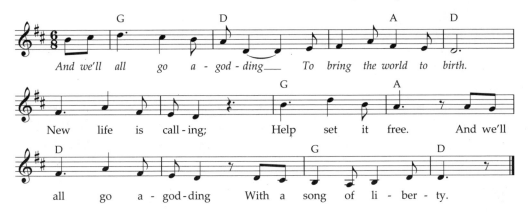

And we'll all go a - god-ding___ To bring the world to birth.

New life is call-ing; Help set it free. And we'll

all go a - god-ding With a song of li - ber - ty.

And we'll all go a-godding
To bring the world to birth.

1 New life is calling;
   Help set it free.
   And we'll all go a-godding
   With a song of liberty.
   Chorus

2 Hunger is calling,
   Find food to share;
   And we'll all go a-godding
   To give out abundant care.
   Chorus

3 Hopelessness calling
   Lonely and drear;
   And we'll all go a-godding
   In warm friendship drawing near.
   Chorus

4 Warfare is calling.
   When will it cease?
   And we'll all go a-godding,
   In our arms, the flowers of peace.
   Chorus

5 Justice is calling,
   Scales in her hand;
   And we'll all go a-godding,
   In her strength we'll take a stand.
   Chorus

6 Wisdom is calling;
   Search out her ways;
   And we'll all go a-godding
   To the ending of our days.
   Chorus

*Goddess theologians, like Carol Christ, have developed the notion of God/Goddess as verb. This
emphasises the divine as activity and process, following the process philosophers and theologians.
I decided to attempt to express this in a song. It was written at Holy Rood House in December
2005, and people who sang it there found it great fun and useful in their lives. One wrote that
faced with a difficult and necessary task she made up a new verse to help her on her way. The text
uses a verbal formation common in the English folk tradition, which has had a great influence on
my work.*

75   Life Cycle

June Boyce-Tillman (1943–)

A time for the birth-ing, a time for the dy-ing,

A time for re-tain-ing, a time to let go, A time for em-

-brac-ing, a time for re-frain-ing, Each seas-on is

com-ing, each seas-on will go. And the cir-cle goes round,

And we're re-cy-cled; And the cir-cle goes round,

And we are healed; And the cir-cle goes round, And we are

strength-ened, In love en-circl-ing, in love en-closed.

1 A time for the birthing, a time for the dying,
   A time for retaining, a time to let go,
   A time for embracing, a time for refraining,
   Each season is coming, each season will go.
   And the circle goes round,
   And we're recycled;
   And the circle goes round,
   And we are healed;
   And the circle goes round,
   And we are strengthened,
   In love encircling, in love enclosed.

2 Sometimes we seem older, sometimes we grow youthful;
   Sometimes we fare badly, sometimes we excel;
   Sometimes we're reflective, sometimes we take action;
   But which are the good times? Who can really tell?
   Chorus

3 A time for aloneness, sometimes we're together,
   A time when the pain comes, a time when it goes;
   A time for remembering and one for forgetting;
   But which bring the good luck? There's One alone knows.
   Chorus

This song is the product of my thinking about the nature of evil that is worked out in a music-theatre piece about Julian and Hildegard entitled 'Exiles'. It shows how difficult it is to judge which are the productive events in our lives. The opera was performed at La Sainte Union College, Southampton, St Mary's, Chard as part of the Chard Festival of Women's Music in 1996, and in Norwich Cathedral at a festival celebrating the religious life, organised by Sister Pamela Owens CAH. It is the theme song of the piece and is sung by the audience with the help of Jack-in-the-green. The text is concerned with the circular nature of our life's journey epitomised by the labyrinth (see No. 162).

76 Spring Song

June Boyce-Tillman (1943–)

Be - hold, I am mak-ing all things new, Feel them spring up with - in you.

-in you. Deep in the rich earth the new life is stir - ring,

stir - ring, stir - ring, stir - ring, E - ner - gy ris - ing is

circl - ing and whirl-ing, whirl-ing, whirl-ing, whirl-ing.

2 Roads are appearing as ways through the wastelands,
Wastelands, wastelands, wastelands,
Rivers are flowing to water the drylands,
Drylands, drylands, drylands.
Chorus

3 Do not look back now, for old wounds are healing,
Healing, healing, healing,
Live in the present, embrace the spring feeling,
Feeling, feeling, feeling.
Chorus

4 Drink deep from fresh streams and sense a new meaning,
Meaning, meaning, meaning.
Dance on the new grass and joy in the greening,
Greening, greening, greening.
Chorus

Based on Isaiah 43, this song was written for Carol Boulter and Womenchurch Reading in March 2004, for a liturgy on spring. This text has been a very significant one for me at the end of spells of depression.

77 Peace Song

June Boyce-Tillman (1943 –)

With strength

Can there be peace when the war-lords rule? Can there be love when the fists are clenched? Can there be hope as the cof-fins fill?_____ Lis - ten,_ __ strug - gle,___ un-der-stand. We are com - mit - ted to work for peace; We are com - mit - ted to work with love; We are com - mit - ted to work with hope; Re-con-ci - ling, me-di-at - ing, un-der-stand-ing.

2 Can there be joy while the tears pour down?
Can we be gentle when dark violence reigns?
Can there be patience when suffering bites?
Listen, struggle, understand.
Chorus

3 Can there be justice for the poor and weak?
Can there be caring for the earth?
Can there be sharing of earthwealth?
Listen, struggle, understand.
Chorus

This was written in 2004 for the International Women's Peace Federation, for my good friends Dolores, Cecilie, Margaret and Tina. It was first sung accompanied by a drum at their Christmas gathering. It forms the basis of a movement in 'Peacesong', first performed in Winchester Cathedral in March 2006. This included 220 adults and 100 children. One teacher commented that singing this song provoked much discussion with her pupils, one of whom said: 'I don't like singing the song but I know they are questions that we need to ask!'

78   Encircling Wisdom

Franz Schubert
arranged June Boyce-Tillman (1943–)

(Ah)

Cir - cling, en - cir - cling   Wis - dom deep with - in,   Gent - ly em - brac - ing

life - giv - ing care, (You are) Cir - cling, en - cir - cling   Wis - dom deep with - in,

We bring you re - ve - rence and   prayer_ to - day.   One wing flies heaven - ward,

Arrangement © Copyright 2006 Stainer & Bell Ltd

one wing flies earth-ward. One wing flies ev - ery - where; You will en-fold us,

you will em-power us, We bring you re-ve-rence and prayer— to - day.

For Paul and Vivienne Light

1   Circling, encircling Wisdom deep within,
    Gently embracing life-giving care, (You are)
    Circling, encircling Wisdom deep within,
    We bring you reverence and prayer today.
    One wing flies heavenward, one wing flies earthward.
    One wing flies everywhere;
    You will enfold us, you will empower us,
    We bring you reverence and prayer today.

continued overleaf

2 Circling, encircling Wisdom deep within,
  Gently embracing life-giving care, (You are)
  Circling, encircling Wisdom deep within,
  We bring you reverence and prayer today.
  Questions of doctrine, moral dilemmas,
  We lay them in your wings.
  Strengthen our weakness, soften our power,
  We bring you reverence and prayer today.

3 Circling, encircling Wisdom deep within,
  Gently embracing life-giving care, (You are)
  Circling, encircling Wisdom deep within,
  We bring you reverence and prayer today.
  Artist's creation, manager's judgement,
  These can reveal your love.
  May all our knowing draw on your values,
  We bring you reverence and prayer today.

4 Circling, encircling Wisdom deep within,
  Gently embracing life-giving care, (You are)
  Circling, encircling Wisdom deep within,
  We bring you reverence and prayer today.
  You are incarnate in our creation;
  In all your glory shines,
  Work with our doubting, challenge our smugness.
  We bring you reverence and prayer today.

The image in verse one, of a three-winged figure of Wisdom, is taken from Hildegard's vision and its associated antiphon, 'O virtus sapientiae'. I have used this to suggest how we are rooted in both heaven and earth, and we need the third wing flowing everywhere to hold these together. This hymn was written for a farewell concert in honour of Paul and Vivienne Light. Paul was Principal/ Vice Chancellor while our college moved from being King Alfred's to the University of Winchester. He was immensely supportive of my work as Director of Foundation Music. This strength transformed my life in the university. In this hymn his 'manager's judgement' is celebrated alongside Viv's 'artist's creation'. She is a fine artist who inspires others. Because I was preoccupied with 'Peacesong', a large-scale cantata performed in March 2006 in Winchester Cathedral, this setting was written on the day of the concert. I heard Schubert's entr'acte from 'Rosamunde' on Classic FM and thought what a fine piece it would make. My good colleague the gifted pianist Diana Owen helped me to recall the harmonies. The text was written in a lay-by at Basingstoke on my regular route between London and Winchester on 21 March 2006. I have found this car journey a good time for creative projects.

79 Ecological Lullaby

June Boyce-Tillman (1943–)

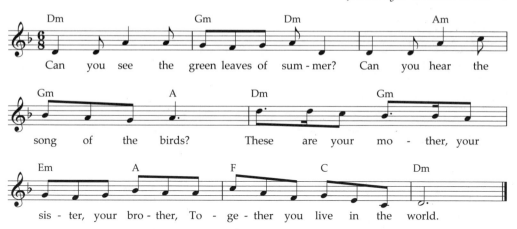

To Scarlett

1 Can you see the green leaves of summer?
   Can you hear the song of the birds?
   These are your mother, your sister, your brother,
   Together you live in the world.

2 Can you taste the honey from beeswax?
   Can you feel the sand with your toes?
   These are your mother, your sister, your brother,
   Together you live in the world.

3 Will you tend the health of the planet?
   Will you guard the trees from the saw?
   These are your mother, your sister, your brother,
   Together you live in the world.

4 When you cross the hills and the valleys
   Will you face them with your truth?
   These are your mother, your sister, your brother,
   Together you live in the world.

There was an internet request for lullabies on ecological themes. I started this, lost it, and then found the opening again when my first grandchild, Scarlett Chloe, was born to my son Matthew and his wife, Andrea, on 9 April 2006.

80 Sacred Endings and Beginnings

June Boyce-Tillman (1943–)

Come, spark-ling wa - ter, in ce - le - bra-tion of a New Year To cleanse our deep wounds_ and pu - ri - fy our lives. Wash a - way, wash a - way All that pre - vents us reach-ing full ma - tu - ri - ty. Ce - le - brate, ce - le - brate sa-cred end - ings and be - gin-nings, Ce - le - -gin-nings.

2 Come, fertile good earth, in celebration of a New Year
To keep us grounded in God's security.
Form our roots, form our roots
That we may firmly stand in all adversity.
Chorus

3 Come, shining candles, in celebration of a New Year
To burn our cold hearts and make them warm with love.
Pierce our eyes, pierce our eyes
That we may see again the wonders of God's world.
Chorus

4 Come, flowing pure air, in celebration of a New Year
To fill our bodies with consecrated health.
Set us free, set us free
That we may breathe again the airy Spirit's power.
Chorus

Like many of my pieces, this song uses the four elements as seminal theological images. It was written in December 1996 at Holy Rood House, Sowerby, run by Elizabeth and Stanley Baxter, and the opening was inspired by Benjamin Britten's 'New Year Carol' from 'Friday Afternoons'. We danced this on 1 January 2000 outside Grace Chapel, Osmotherly, where the Benedictine brothers of Ampleforth Abbey offered us welcome hospitality.

81 Coming Home

Traditional
adapted June Boyce-Tillman (1943–)

Dance in the shoes you're wear - ing, Bloom in the place you're plant - ed,

Dance in the shoes you're wear - ing, There you'll find my joy.

You'll find the love in laugh - ter, Deep in a heart that's sing - ing,

You'll find the love in laugh - ter, When you look with - in.

Dance in the shoes you're wearing,
Bloom in the place you're planted,
Dance in the shoes you're wearing,
There you'll find my joy.

1 You'll find the love in laughter,
Deep in a heart that's singing,
You'll find the love in laughter,
When you look within.
Chorus

2 You'll find the hope in freedom,
Deep in a heart that's singing,
You'll find the hope in freedom,
When you look within.
Chorus

3 You'll find the strength of courage,
Deep in a heart that's singing,
You'll find the strength of courage,
When you look within.
Chorus

Based on traditional proverbs, this song was written with Nancy and Robert in Chetycamp, Nova Scotia in August 2005. They are long-standing friends, who are both artists. 'Blessing Song' (No. 97) was written for their daughter Juda. With them, I have found many treasures in myself, many costumes for my shows, and the beautiful windchimes that underpin my cantata 'Peacesong'. I often dream of a life that is different from the one I have been given. This song is an antidote to this.

82 Love's Energy

June Boyce-Tillman (1943–)

1. Deep in creation's heart an energy
   Calls to us but leaves us free.
   Dance with that universal energy,
   Celebrate life's mystery.

2. Hold out your hands, embrace that energy,
   Love that will not let us go.
   Let loose the bonds that bind that energy,
   Let the streams of mercy flow.

3. Watch how the world takes up that energy;
   Seasons change in rhythmic dance.
   Ebbing and flowing, tidal energy,
   Love in weariness enhance.

4. Boundless supplies there are of energy
   Strengthening us in loving ways.
   Changeless, dynamic, vital energy,
   Dance within us all our days.

This was written in February 1993, after a serious accident, for my own personal use in the midday office. It is intended to be strong, and it can be sung unaccompanied, or with a drum accompaniment and a stamping dance. The tune is dedicated to my homeopath Max Wilkins (who took over from Dr Wendy Singer), who has healed so many of my wounds with 'love's energy'. It is the theme song for my one-woman performance 'Lunacy or the Pursuit of the Goddess'.

83 Element Song

June Boyce-Tillman (1943–)

1 Earth is our humanity,
  Touch it, feel it,
  Cut the flax and crush the oil,
  Touch it, feel it.
  Now is the time for strength and struggle.

2 Water means emotion,
  Taste it, hear it,
  Health and flow and empathy,
  Taste it, feel it.
  Now is the time for hope and integrity.

3 Air of creativity,
  Breathe it, smell it,
  Strengthen our commitment,
  Breathe it, smell it.
  Now is the time for truth and justice.

4 Fire is of the spirit,
  Smell it, watch it,
  Yearning for transcendence,
  Smell it, watch it.
  Now is the time for purpose and action.

I wrote this song for the 1999 WISE Women's Synod, in Liverpool. It was composed for a liturgy using all our senses, devised by Lala Winkley with whom I have co-operated many times liturgically.

84 Mother and Daughter

June Boyce-Tillman (1943–)

Flesh of one flesh, once joined to-ge-ther, Mo-ther and daugh-ter, what do you fear? Life in its rich-ness has thrown you to-ge-ther, Mo-ther and daugh-ter, you are so near. What can I say of your liv-ing to-ge-ther? How can I speak from the depth of my heart? How forge the song from the flows and the ed-dies In such a mael-strom, where can I start?

For Nellie

Flesh of one flesh, once joined together,
Mother and daughter, what do you fear?
Life in its richness has thrown you together,
Mother and daughter, you are so near.

1 What can I say of your living together?
   How can I speak from the depth of my heart?
   How forge the song from the flows and the eddies
   In such a maelstrom, where can I start?
   Chorus

2 I would remember the colours of autumn,
   Treading the beech mast and crunching the snow,
   Presents at Christmas and smelling the lilac,
   Sweetness in trifles and water's soft flow.
   Chorus

3 Time is erasing the times of the weeping,
   Loving turned crazy and tears that won't cry,
   Raging and storming and knots of endurance,
   Times in the dark and the breath that won't sigh.
   Chorus

4 We were both caught in a chain of misusings,
   Trapped women's talents in houses too small,
   Bodies mishandled and murmuring madness;
   Can we break free from what held us in thrall?
   Chorus

5 Now we are separate, living's turned easy.
   I find forgiveness in wounds that can heal.
   Now we can look in the face of the other;
   This then is your song to say how I feel.
   Chorus

This was written in May 2005 in an open-air paella café in Madrid. I was at a conference designed to produce a book on peace-making and music, chaired by Olivier Urbain. Rik Palieri, a colleague of the protest singer Pete Seeger, had talked about how he had achieved a reconciliation with his father by composing a song that he sang at a family gathering. My mother is dead, but I thought I might achieve a measure of resolution of our complex and troubled relationship by means of a song. In verse four there is a reference to Ibsen's 'The Doll's House' and how my mother's generation were trapped in a particular form of marriage. This meant that often all of a woman's energy was focussed on one small group of people. The song forms part of my one-woman performance 'Juggling – A Question of Identity'. It is sung as a letter to her, and has moved many others who can identify with it.

85   The Anointing

June Boyce-Tillman (1943–)

1   Give thou to me, O God,
    The healing power of oil.
    Give thou to me, O God,
    A place beside the healer of my soul;
    Give thou to me, O God,
    A death with joy and peace.

2   Give thou to me, O God,
    To know the death of Christ;
    Give thou to me, O God,
    That I may contemplate Christ's agony;
    Give thou to me, O God,
    To warm with love of Christ.

3 O thou great God of heaven,
    Draw thou my soul to thee,
    That I repent aright
    With upright, strengthened, pure and straightened heart,
    A broken heart, contrite,
    That shall not bend nor yield.

4 Of angels, thou art God.
    Bring me to dwell in peace.
    Of angels, thou art God.
    Preserve me from all evil magic charms.
    Of angels, thou art God,
    Please bathe me in thy pool.

The original version was written in July 1986 and based on a text by Ann MacDonald in 'Carmina Gadelica'. The opening lines were then: 'Give thou to me, O God, The death of the priceless oils.' It was first sung to a different tune as an introit in St Paul's Church, Tooting. It was revised and this tune was written for a Eucharist for the healing of the wounds of child abuse, held at St Michael's Convent, Ham Common, on 14 March 1992. It was beautifully sung as part of this by Sister Aileen CSC, while my good friend and healer, Pat Macey, mixed the oils for the anointing that was part of the liturgy. It has since been used for many services of healing in the United Kingdom, USA and Canada, and recorded on the CDs 'Voice of Experience' and 'Singing the Mystery – Hildegard Revisited'. The Community of the Sisters of the Church (with whom I am an associate) have been wonderfully supportive on my creative journey. It was in their beautiful chapel where my hymns have been sung that I took several limited vows of celibacy following my divorce. For my thinking about angels see No. 127.

86 Contemplation

June Boyce-Tillman (1943–)

Fall in-to the still-ness, Fall in-to the still-ness,

Fall in-to the still-ness, My arms will hold you.

Form a circle by joining hands around the backs of one another. For line one, take one step right and close. For line two, take one step left and close. For line three, sway to the right, then to the left. For line four, lean out resting on the joined hands.

1   Fall into the stillness,
    Fall into the stillness,
    Fall into the stillness,
    My arms will hold you.

2   Let my arms enfold you,
    Let my arms enfold you,
    Let my arms enfold you,
    Your body relaxed.

3   Letting go the tensions,
    Letting go the tensions,
    Letting go the tensions,
    My peace will flow through.

4   Peace is flowing through you,
    Peace is flowing through you,
    Peace is flowing through you,
    And stilling your soul.

A circular song, which can be repeated several times. It has been used to start many retreats. I wrote it as an introduction to a period of silence, and it was first tried out as a dance with the liturgy group which met at the Deanery, Southampton, in February 1995. This house has meant a great deal to me at several points in my life. When Roy Chamberlain was the vicar there, he and his wife Eileen entertained me every Sunday for breakfast and supported my adolescent journey out of my family. In the hands of Gillian Lamb and Sue Orton, it again proved a source of strength on many occasions. It was developed as a centre for urban prayer by my good friends Joan and David Perkins, whose study group helped me develop my ideas as an adolescent in the choir of St Mary's, Southampton, with the Rev. Sir John Alleyne.

87 A Song for Caedmon's Cross

June Boyce-Tillman (1943–)

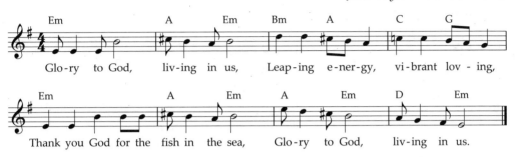

Glo-ry to God, liv-ing in us, Leap-ing e-ner-gy, vi-brant lov - ing,
Thank you God for the fish in the sea, Glo-ry to God, liv-ing in us.

For Elizabeth and Stanley

Glory to God, living in us,
Leaping energy, vibrant loving,
Thank you God for the fish in the sea,
Glory to God, living in us.

This was written for my friends Elizabeth and Stanley Baxter, who were in co-operation with English Heritage, building services at the Celtic crosses in Yorkshire during Lent 2003. I preached at the cross at Whitby on a glorious day with a deep blue sea and seagulls wheeling and calling. It was a magical experience. The song is intended to be extended by substituting other animals, people or parts of the natural world for 'fish in the sea' to create more verses. Children did this on that day in Whitby. I realised how easy it is to preach when you have the natural world close to you and people all around you.

88 Julian's Prayer

June Boyce-Tillman (1943–)

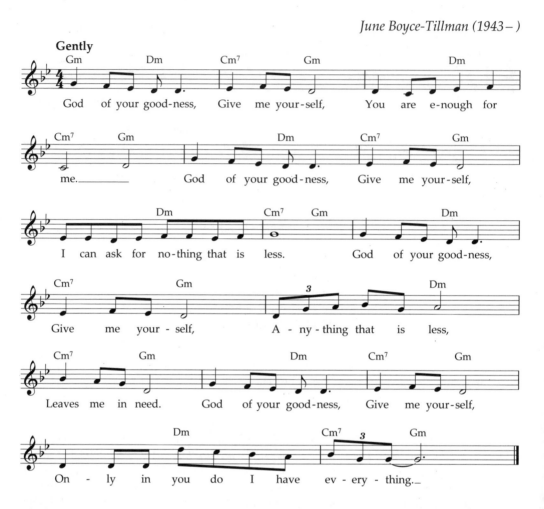

The first two bars may be sung throughout the piece as an ostinato with the repeated chord sequence Gm Dm Cm7 Gm, while others sing the whole tune.

1 God of your goodness,
   Give me yourself,
   You are enough for me.
   God of your goodness,
   Give me yourself,
   I can ask for nothing that is less.

2 God of your goodness,
   Give me yourself,
   Anything that is less,
   Leaves me in need.
   God of your goodness,
   Give me yourself,
   Only in you do I have everything.

This was written as part of my one-person show based on Julian of Norwich, where it is the recurring refrain. It also features in 'Exiles', my opera based on Hildegard and Julian.

89 The Vision

June Boyce-Tillman (1943–)

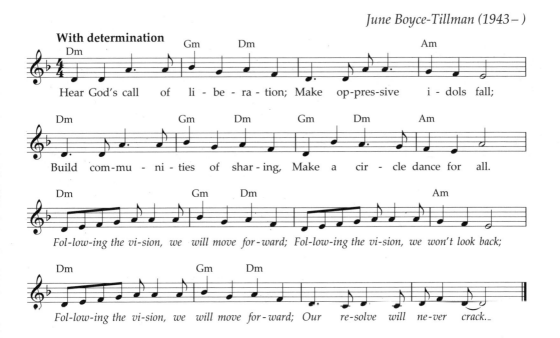

For Myra

1 Hear God's call of liberation;
   Make oppressive idols fall;
   Build communities of sharing,
   Make a circle dance for all.
   Following the vision, we will move forward;
   Following the vision, we won't look back;
   Following the vision, we will move forward;
   Our resolve will never crack.

2 Hear the vision of our leaders;
   Feel the strength we all can share;
   Claim the power of Wisdom's women;
   Make a circle dance of care.
   Chorus

This song (which developed into No. 113) was written in 2003, for Myra Poole's birthday. It celebrates her tireless work for Catholic Women's Ordination. She has risked everything for her vision. The last line of the chorus can be repeated as many times as you wish.

90 Birth Song

June Boyce-Tillman (1943–)

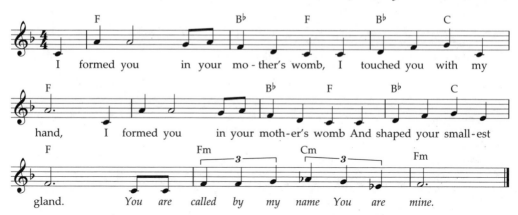

I formed you in your mo-ther's womb, I touched you with my hand, I formed you in your moth-er's womb And shaped your small-est gland. *You are called by my name You are mine.*

2 I formed you in your mother's womb,
I held you on the wave,
I formed you in your mother's womb
Gave you the love you crave.
Chorus

3 I formed you in your mother's womb,
I made your limbs unfold,
I formed you in your mother's womb
And shaped you in my mould.
Chorus

4 I formed you in your mother's womb,
I guided your escape,
I formed you in your mother's womb
And etched in you my shape.
Chorus

5 I formed you in your mother's womb,
I made you with my earth,
I formed you in your mother's womb
And whispered at your birth.
Chorus

This song, based on Isaiah 44:24 and 43:1, was written on 10 November 2005, and is dedicated to Lady Bronwen Astor. I have long used the chorus as an affirming mantra in my meditation practice. I was born three months premature during the war, and the relationship with my birth family was complicated. But my rebirthing experience was one of encounter with God's all-embracing love and I am grateful to Bronwen for this. Interestingly, the song was written before the experience and prefigures what happened.

91 Liberation

June Boyce-Tillman (1943–)

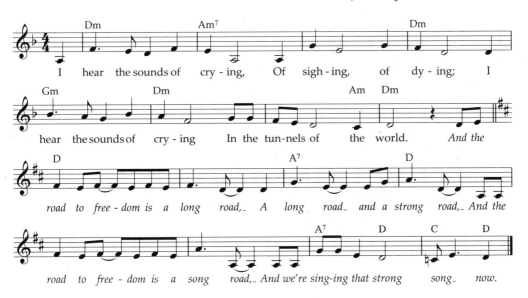

I hear the sounds of cry-ing, Of sigh-ing, of dy-ing; I hear the sounds of cry-ing In the tun-nels of the world. And the road to free-dom is a long road,_ A long road_ and a strong road,_ And the road to free-dom is a song road,_ And we're sing-ing that strong song_ now.

1 I hear the sounds of crying,
   Of sighing, of dying;
   I hear the sounds of crying
   In the tunnels of the world.
   And the road to freedom is a long road,
   A long road and a strong road,
   And the road to freedom is a song road,
   And we're singing that strong song now.

2 I see the signs of weeping,
   Infected wounds are seeping;
   I see the signs of weeping
   In the bowels of the soil.
   Chorus

3 I smell the stench of oppression,
   Obsession, repression;
   I smell the stench of oppression
   In the corridors of power.
   Chorus

4 I taste the bitter living,
   The sweetness of forgiving,
   The bitter-sweet taste of living
   In the lifeblood of the land.
   Chorus

5 I sense a warmth of feeling,
   The soothing touch of healing;
   I sense the warmth of feeling
   In the wellsprings of the earth.
   Chorus

Written in June 2001 as a 60th-birthday present for Mary Grey, this song reflects the concerns of a leading ecotheologian. It also features as the first underworld descent in my performance 'Lunacy or the Pursuit of the Goddess', where it is sung to powerful effect under a purple blanket, which in the show represents the underworld.

92 Been There, Done That

Traditional
arranged June Boyce-Tillman (1943 –)

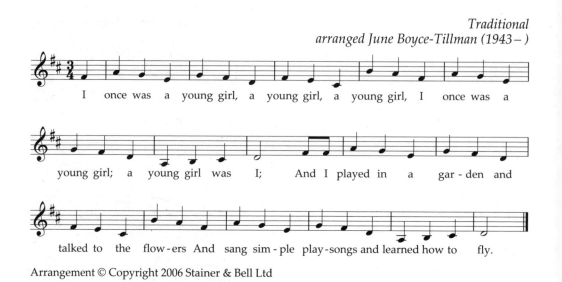

I once was a young girl, a young girl, a young girl, I once was a
young girl; a young girl was I; And I played in a gar-den and
talked to the flow-ers And sang sim-ple play-songs and learned how to fly.

1 I once was a young girl, a young girl, a young girl,
  I once was a young girl; a young girl was I;
  And I played in a garden and talked to the flowers
  And sang simple play songs and learned how to fly.

2 I once was a daughter, a daughter, a daughter,
  I once was a daughter; a daughter was I;
  And I bowed to my parents and served them with honour
  And gave them devotion and learned how to cry.

3 I once was a pupil, a pupil, a pupil,
  I once was a pupil; a pupil was I;
  And I worked at my studies and I slaved at my learning,
  Bent over my book desk and learned how to try.

4 I once was a teacher, a teacher, a teacher,
  I once was a teacher; a teacher was I;
  And I nurtured my pupils, supported their footsteps,
  And taught them in learning to always ask why.

5 I once was a true love, a true love, a true love,
   I once was a true love; a true love was I;
   And I longed for him, trusted and gave him my body
   And vowed I would stay with him till I should die.

6 I once was a mother, a mother, a mother,
   I once was a mother; a mother was I;
   And I nurtured my children with joy and with loving
   Said: 'Come to me freely. Your needs I'll supply.'

7 I once was a good wife, a good wife, a good wife,
   I once was a good wife; a good wife was I;
   And I cared for my family with love and devotion
   And when danger threatened was standing close by.

8 I once was a lost wife, a lost wife, a lost wife,
   I once was a lost wife; a lost wife was I;
   And I learned about jealousy, envy and hatred
   And loving turned sour and tears that won't cry.

9 And now I'm a woman, a woman, a woman,
   And now I'm a woman; a woman am I;
   I'll abandon my striving to meet expectations
   And stay true to my own Wisdom's wealth till I die.

To celebrate some of the things I have learnt in my life I wrote this song in 1994, basing the music on a child's rhyme. It also forms the basis of 'Juggling – A Question of Identity', a performance-piece about the roles we have to play. It reflects my thinking on multiple identities (see Introduction) and how women learn a number of performances that shape their identity. The last verse is a particular favourite of my good friend Sue Williamson, who has used a number of my pieces in various publications.

93 God the Artist

June Boyce-Tillman (1943 –)

Happily

I want to make a rain-bow And paint it with my love,___ But

first I'll make the paint-box, Link earth with heaven a-bove.___ I'll

start off with the dark end And move to-wards the light,___ Then

blend them all___ to-ge-ther To make a light that's white.___ We're

rid-ing on a rain-bow, We're rid-ing on a rain-bow, We're

rid-ing on a rain-bow, That tells us of God's love.___

1 I want to make a rainbow
And paint it with my love,
But first I'll make the paintbox,
Link earth with heaven above.
I'll start off with the dark end
And move towards the light,
Then blend them all together
To make a light that's white.
We're riding on a rainbow,
We're riding on a rainbow,
We're riding on a rainbow,
That tells us of God's love.

2 So first I'll make the violet
  By touching purple shoots;
  The indigo takes longer –
  I'll need some deep, dark roots;
  The green will not be too hard –
  Just wait till spring begins;
  For blue I'll need some water
  And flashing fishy fins.
  Chorus

3 The yellow lies on the seashore
  And glows in summer sun;
  The oranges have ripened,
  Now autumn has begun;
  The red I'll find in winter
  In berries on the tree.
  With these I'll paint a picture
  That you'll delight to see.
  Chorus

4 For there's another canvas
  That isn't in the sky,
  A space in every person,
  A heart where tears can cry,
  A place where joy can spring up
  Like sunshine after rain,
  A gentle, creamy paper,
  Where I can paint again.
  Chorus

5 I'll use those same old colours
  With which I paint the sky,
  Remind them of the promise
  I made in years gone by,
  Recall in them my loving,
  My caring for my world,
  Each time they see the rainbow
  Across the earth unfurled.
  Chorus

The Rev. Marian Carter offered me much warm friendship and hospitality when I first worked at King Alfred's College, Winchester, and this song was written for her at St Mary's Abbey, West Malling in January 1991. It was used as the theme song for her Rainbow People holiday project. It was sung by the children of the church of St Mark, Kempshott with Hatch Warren, Basingstoke, at her ordination there as deacon on 29 March 1992. By using the first person, it represents a further experiment in inclusive language for God.

94   A Gaelic Lullaby

June Boyce-Tillman (1943–)

I wrap my body and soul within The cloak of thy guarding this night,— O bride, Calm nurse-mo-ther to Christ with-out sin, Lov - er of Christ of the wound - ed side.

2 I wrap my soul and body so sure,
   With the cloak of the guarding of Mary so dear,
   Mighty protector of heaven and earth,
   Mother of Christ of the sorrowful tear.

3 I wrap my soul and my body from fears
   With the cloak of thy guarding, O Christ, this night,
   Piercéd son of the wounds and the tears,
   Under thy cross may all be made right.

4 I wrap my soul and my body so sure,
   With the cloak of thy guarding, O God, this night,
   Loving Father to all the world's poor,
   May you protect earth and heaven this night.

The bride referred to in the text is St Brigid of Ireland, a Celtic saint (see also No. 55), and the text draws on Celtic sources. It was finished in June 1992 for the profession of Sister Aileen SSC, who has given me so much support. The use of the wrapping image for God links with the thinking of Julian of Norwich.

Transfiguration Hymn

June Boyce-Tillman (1943–)

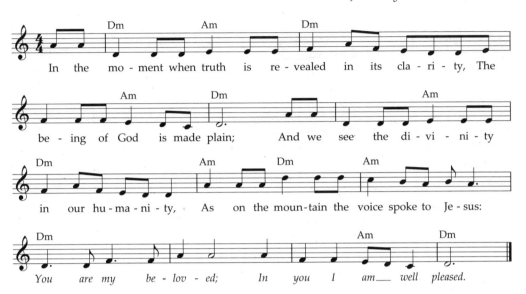

1 In the moment when truth is revealed in its clarity,
   The being of God is made plain;
   And we see the divinity in our humanity,
   As on the mountain the voice spoke to Jesus:
   You are my beloved;
   In you I am well pleased.

2 In the moment when hope lights the struggle of true prayer
   Discerning the course of our life,
   We can see in the chaos the answer lies there,
   As on the mountain the voice said to Jesus:
   Chorus

3 In the moment of sensing your strong arms enfold us,
   We know we are loved as we are;
   In the deepest acceptance we know that you hold us,
   And from within we can hear your voice saying:
   Chorus

Written in August 2001 at Prasada for my good friends Sisters Jean and Cecile CGA, this links the transfiguration with God's affirmation in our own lives. It was used powerfully in a sermon at St James's, Piccadilly where the Rev. Charles Hedley was so supportive of my ministry during my ordination training. I try to use a song in all my sermons, especially one with a chorus. People find it a helpful way of taking something memorable home with them for use during the week.

96   Wisdom Song

June Boyce-Tillman (1943–)

In the de - sert Wis - dom is call - ing,_____ Where the
earth's deep - est well - springs are cry - ing._____ She says
'Spread out my blan - ket of mer - cy_____ To breathe my life in - to the
dy - ing.' I will go, God, if you will re - make me. I will
fol - low if you will re - make me. You are my mo - ther, my
sis - ter, my bro - ther. I will join in re - mak - ing the world.

1 In the desert Wisdom is calling,
   Where the earth's deepest wellsprings are crying.
   She says: 'Spread out my blanket of mercy
   To breathe my life into the dying.'
   I will go, God, if you will remake me.
   I will follow if you will remake me.
   You are my mother, my sister, my brother.
   I will join in remaking the world.

2   In the market Wisdom is calling,
    In the rhythm of selling and buying;
    She says: 'Take up the hammer of justice
    To breathe my life into the dying.'
    Chorus

3   In the classroom Wisdom is calling,
    When the paradigms are stultifying;
    She says: 'Put on my sword-belt of knowing
    To breathe my life into the dying.'
    Chorus

4   In the oratory Wisdom is calling,
    She says: 'My food is revivifying.
    Feed from my body and drink of my blood
    To breathe my life into the dying.'
    Chorus

I wrote this text for the ordination of the Rt Rev. Professor Elizabeth Stuart at the Unitarian Church, Southampton on 25 September 2001. I also sang it at her consecration as bishop in the Open Episcopal Church in the chapel of Royal Holloway College on 10 April 2003. It reflects aspects of her life: her concern for ecotheology and for justice, her challenging theology and the centrality of the Eucharistic celebration to her life. I have stayed with her often while working at the University of Winchester and have so enjoyed her celebration of the Mass.

97 Blessing Song

For Juda

June Boyce-Tillman (1943–)

Ju - da, Ju - da, Life will move you with its ebb and flow.

Ju - da, Ju - da, May the power be with you as you go. May the

air sup - port_ you As you take your flight; May the earth mas-

-sage_ you And hold you tight; May the sun warm you gent-ly And the

waves give you strength; And may love sur-round you soft - ly In bright-ening day___

___ and calm - ing night. Ju - da, Ju - da,

Life will move you with its ebb and flow. May the power be with you as you go.

This was written in 1999 for the Bat Mitzvah of Juda, daughter of my good friends Nancy Winternight and Robert Selkowitz in Cape Breton, Nova Scotia (see No. 81). Nancy and Robert have given me warm hospitality on many occasions in Canada and the USA. I have learned a great deal about angels and channelling from Nancy. The song could be used for any blessing, including baptism or confirmation, by substituting a new name for Juda.

98 Peace Prayer

June Boyce-Tillman (1943–)

The last four bars can be repeated throughout as an ostinato, with the following chord sequence:

‖: Bm F♯m | Bm | Em⁷ F♯m | Bm :‖

Lead us from death to life, from falsehood to truth.
Lead us from despair to hope, from fear to trust.
Lead us from hate to love, from war to peace.
Let peace fill our hearts, fill our world, fill our universe.
Peace, peace, peace. Peace, peace, peace.

This tune and text have been used at the annual interfaith gathering held at St Paul's, Furzedown since 1984. This has enabled me to form links with local Muslims, Sikhs, Jews, Buddhists, Unificationists and Hindus. I feel very drawn to this ministry as a counterbalance to the media's presentation of interfaith dialogue as deriving from violence and force. The piece forms the basis of a movement in my cantata 'Peacesong'. This song has been used in the regular interfaith gatherings at St Paul's, Furzedown. I have organised these since 1986. They are always a challenge but the rewards are to bring the faiths together in a society which seems to think that all interfaith dialogue is done at the end of a gun.

99   Let Nothing Disturb You

June Boyce-Tillman (1943–)

The first two bars can be repeated throughout the piece as an ostinato, with the repeated chord sequence: G Bm⁷ Cmaj⁷ D. At the end the final D chord is replaced by a G.

> Let nothing disturb you, nothing cause you fear.
> All things are passing; God is unchanging.
> Let nothing disturb you, nothing cause you fear.
> Patience obtains all; wait in expectation.
> Let nothing disturb you, nothing cause you fear.
> Whoever has God needs nothing else.
> Let nothing disturb you, nothing cause you fear.
> God alone will be sufficient.

I have learned a great deal in my prayer life from St Teresa of Avila's classic 'The Interior Castle'. She has enabled me to construct my own interior landscape. Her prayer is very important to me and is in many ways complementary to Julian of Norwich's prayer (No. 88). The chords here are a major version of those underpinning Julian's prayer.

100 Communion Song

June Boyce-Tillman (1943–)

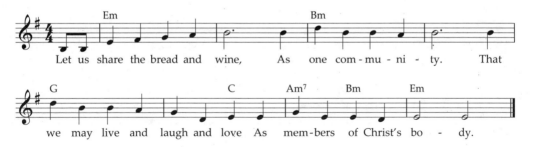

Let us share the bread and wine, As one com-mu-ni-ty. That we may live and laugh and love As mem-bers of Christ's bo - dy.

1 Let us share the bread and wine,
   As one community.
   That we may live and laugh and love
   As members of Christ's body.

2 Let us share this family meal
   As Jesus did with friends,
   That earth wounds may be touched and healed
   And we can make amends.

3 Now the heavenly hosts draw near;
   We sense their guarding love
   And feeling gentle wings around
   We draw strength from above.

This was written for one of the many ecumenical gatherings at Ianthe Pratt's house. She has the capacity for drawing different people together and forming them into a coherent group by her hospitality.

101   A Song of God's Creation

June Boyce-Tillman (1943–)

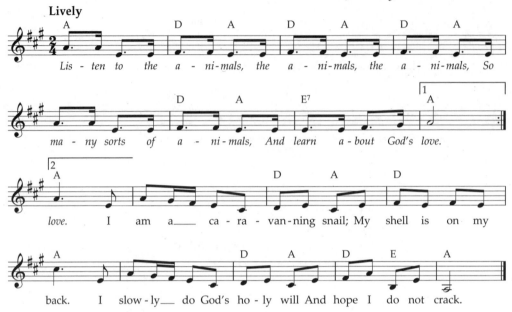

Lis - ten to the a - ni - mals, the a - ni - mals, the a - ni - mals, So

ma - ny sorts of a - ni - mals, And learn a - bout God's love.

love.   I   am   a___ ca - ra - van-ning snail; My shell is on my

back.   I   slow - ly___ do God's ho - ly will And hope I do not crack.

Listen to the animals, the animals, the animals,
So many sorts of animals,
And learn about God's love.
Listen to the animals, the animals, the animals,
So many sorts of animals,
And learn about God's love.

1   I am a caravanning snail;
    My shell is on my back.
    I slowly do God's holy will
    And hope I do not crack.
    Listen to the tiny snail, the tiny snail, the tiny snail,
    Just listen to the tiny snail,
    And learn about God's love.
    Listen to the animals, the animals, the animals,
    So many sorts of animals,
    And learn about God's love.

2   A leaping, prancing mountain goat,
    I take a lot of risks.
    My love of life and faith in God
    Have some precariousness.
    Listen to the mountain goat ...

3　I am a gently waddling duck,
　　Of all the birds the clown,
　　I have a hoarsely quacking laugh
　　A sadness-cracking sound.
　　Listen to the waddling duck ...

4　The bees all zoom from flower to flower,
　　Like missiles on the wing;
　　God gave us so much work to do;
　　Disturb us and we sting!
　　Listen to the zooming bees ...

5　The mighty golden eagle soars
　　Above the mountain peaks.
　　I gaze upon the earth below
　　And all God's tiny beasts.
　　Listen to the mighty eagle ...

7　The lion is king of all the beasts;
　　I give a mighty roar.
　　Please try not to be scared of me
　　But bravely love me more.
　　Listen to the mighty lion ...

6　The earthworm quietly works away
　　In tunnels, tubes and holes,
　　To play a small essential part
　　In God's tremendous goals.
　　Listen to the quiet worm ...

8　The dinosaurs arrived, then went,
　　But we still carried on;
　　For tortoises are steadfast folk;
　　We know God's time is long.
　　Listen to the tortoises ...

9　Mosquitoes dancing in the dusk
　　Rise up and fall in flight,
　　We try to carry out God's plan;
　　Forgive us if we bite.
　　Watch mosquitoes as they dance ...

10　So many different shapes and kinds
　　In feather, fur or shell,
　　We living creatures clearly show
　　That God made all things well.
　　Listen to the animals ...

This was written at St Mary's Abbey, West Malling in January 1992 for a project book entitled 'All Creatures Great and Small' by the Rev. Marian Carter, and published by the National Christian Education Council. It draws on my long experience (some forty years) of writing songs for children.

102   Angel Dance

June Boyce-Tillman (1943 –)

For Lillalou

Lillalou angel with greening and dancing,
Lillalou angel encircle with love.
Lillalou angel with greening and dancing,
Lillalou angel encircle with love.
Bright are the shining ones,
Weaving the earth dance,
Vibrant with energy,
Circling the world.

For the birthday of my friend Lillalou Hughes, who has done so much for the Britain and Ireland School of Feminist Theology, I wrote this song, which reflects her love of circle-dancing and angels. They are very important in my thinking and they are present in most religious traditions, including the so-called New Age. I feel their presence very strongly in prayer and I use them in my intercessions. The Rt Rev. Professor Elizabeth Stuart has taught me a great deal about their presence at the Eucharist (see No. 127).

103   The Blessing of Light

June Boyce-Tillman (1943–)

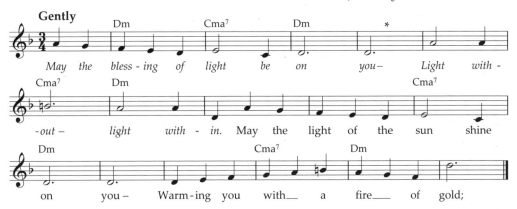

May the bless-ing of light be on you – Light with-
-out – light with - in. May the light of the sun shine
on you – Warm-ing you with a fire of gold;

This may be sung as a round. The second part starts at the *. You can use the chorus and verse as a basis for a series of liturgical actions with a group of people who have learnt to trust one another. Stand in a circle as for a grand chain, each person facing one person next to them and with their back to the other. In line one touch your partner's right cheek with your right hand and then the left cheek with the left hand. In line two with palms facing your partner draw a circle away from your body, first out of the circle and then into the circle. On line one of the verse allow the palms to touch flat together and circle both palms simultaneously in a big circle away from the body. In line two of the verse take right hands and passing right shoulders move to face next partner.

> *May the blessing of light be on you –*
> *Light without – light within.*

1 May the light of the sun shine on you –
    Warming you with a fire of gold;
    Chorus

2 May the light of the moon caress you –
    Calming your mind in a dreamless sleep;
    Chorus

3 May the light of the stars smile on you –
    Lifting your heart to thoughts above;
    Chorus

4 May the light in your soul speak gently –
    Guiding your feet in the ways of love;
    Chorus

Cecily Taylor

'The Blessing of Light' was a present from Cecily Taylor for my fiftieth birthday, made in a beautiful candle-shaped card. I have valued my long association with Cecily's work which started in the 1970s through our link with Stainer & Bell. The piece ends my one-woman performance on Margery Kempe – 'The Gift of Tears'.

104　Letting Go

June Boyce-Tillman (1943–)

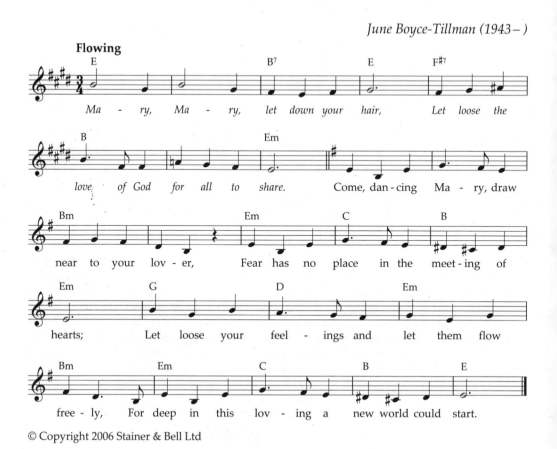

Flowing

Ma - ry, Ma - ry, let down your hair, Let loose the
love of God for all to share. Come, dan - cing Ma - ry, draw
near to your lov - er, Fear has no place in the meet - ing of
hearts; Let loose your feel - ings and let them flow
free - ly, For deep in this lov - ing a new world could start.

To Sandra Pollerman

Mary, Mary, let down your hair,
Let loose the love of God for all to share.

1　Come, dancing Mary, draw near to your lover,
　Fear has no place in the meeting of hearts;
　Let loose your feelings and let them flow freely,
　For deep in this loving a new world could start.
　Chorus

2　Tight is the binding that braids your hair closely;
　Tight are the bonds that are locking your heart;
　Tight is your clothing and tight is your living,
　And tight is the terror from which your life starts.
　Chorus

3   Grieving is over and springtime is coming,
    Here in the garden the new shoots appear;
    Those binding bonds are the frosts of the winter;
    Let love burn its way through the ice of your fear.
    Chorus

4   See how your lover advances in springtime;
    Throw your arms widely in passion's embrace;
    Look in the eyes that are longing to meet you,
    And hold up your head; you can meet face to face.
    Chorus

5   All of your life you have lived in fear's prison,
    Made in a world that has sharpened your pain;
    See it is over, it's time to start living;
    A human shape beckons, start dancing again.
    Chorus

For a liturgy of Mary Magdalene in November 1994, arranged by Ianthe Pratt for the Wimbledon Liturgy Group to whom I owe so much, I wrote this song, in which Mary can be taken as Mary Magdalene or as a name for any woman (as in the black spiritual tradition). The dedicatee, Sandra Pollerman, heard it at the gathering, and it is to her that I owe the discovery of my clowns Isabella and Flombow. After years of depression I encountered the group called 'The Holy Fools' who clown in liturgy. This enabled me to find a real joy inside of me through creating two clown personas, one male, one female. It was Sandra who guided me to this as we gradually developed her costume, her white face and her bobbing asymmetric hair bunches. The song itself is about freedom, here symbolised by the letting down of the hair. This is a powerful symbol for women, as in some cultures, loose hair signifies an available woman while married women's hair must be tightly bound. I wrote this song on a bus from Norwich where I was staying at the Julian cell (which has been so important in my life). It was a time when I felt parts of me that had been frozen were beginning to come to life again, a little like the children's classic 'The Secret Garden' by Frances Hodgson Burnett (used by Nicola Slee for a beautiful Easter meditation book). 'Letting Go' was written long before Dan Brown wrote 'The Da Vinci Code'!

105 The Rucksack of God

June Boyce-Tillman (1943–)

Mov-ing   on,   mov-ing   on,   we must   keep   on   mov-ing   on,   For the

Spi – rit   is   call – ing   us   on;   We   must   walk   the   God   walk,   we   must

talk   the   God   talk,   As   we   keep   up   our   mov – ing   a – long.

For Stanley Baxter

Moving on, moving on, we must keep on moving on,
For the Spirit is calling us on;
We must walk the God walk, we must talk the God talk,
As we keep up our moving along.

1 We must pack in the sack that we bear on our back
   (For the Spirit is calling us on)
   All the things we will need to walk on at God's speed,
   As we keep up our moving along.
   Chorus

2 Pack the chocolate of hope that will help us to cope,
   (For the Spirit is calling us on)
   And the sparkling glühwein that will make us all shine,
   As we keep up our moving along.
   Chorus

3 Now a walking stick of strength will take up the whole bag's length,
   (For the Spirit is calling us on)
   But it keeps our walk tough when the going is rough,
   As we keep up our moving along.
   Chorus

4 Pack the Joybook of Jokes that's for cheering up folks
(For the Spirit is calling us on)
And a duvet of hugs to protect us from bugs,
As we keep up our moving along.
Chorus

5 Pack the massaging oil that will help with the toil
(For the Spirit is calling us on)
And a prayer for God's care when we face our despair,
As we keep up our moving along.
Chorus

6 Pack the small mobile phone for those calls to our home;
(For the Spirit is calling us on)
For we need many friends when we're going round the bend
As we keep up our moving along.
Chorus

7 Pack a spare angel wing and a choir that can sing,
(For the Spirit is calling us on)
For some good angel cheer makes the heaven path clear,
As we keep up our moving along.
Chorus

This was written for the Rev. Stanley Baxter's 70th birthday in 2001 and was sung first (to the surprise of the other diners) in a café in north London. It draws on images from his life: a walking stick, food, jokes, his respect for alternative therapies. His life has been very varied and there is a pilgrimage quality in the image of the rucksack.

106 God in Relationship

June Boyce-Tillman (1943–)

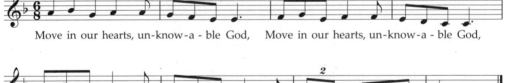

Move in our hearts, un-know-a-ble God,   Move in our hearts, un-know-a-ble God,

Move in our hearts, un-know-a-ble God,   Be with us   while_   we pray.

For Robert Kaggwa

1 Move in our hearts, unknowable God,
   Move in our hearts, unknowable God,
   Move in our hearts, unknowable God,
   Be with us while we pray.

2 You were made known in Jesus's life,
   You were made known in Jesus's life,
   You were made known in Jesus's life,
   Be with us while we pray.

3 Each of us has a part of the truth,
   Each of us has a part of the truth,
   Each of us has a part of the truth,
   Be with us while we pray.

4 May we draw near with love and respect,
   May we draw near with love and respect,
   May we draw near with love and respect,
   Be with us while we pray.

5 We can all fit together in you,
   We can all fit together in you,
   We can all fit together in you,
   Be with us while we pray.

This was written for the same event as No. 59. For me the important thing about faith is that God is unknowable and this is the ultimate guard against human arrogance. It means that the person before us always has the possibility of having parts of the truth that we have not yet perceived. This is a recipe for respect. This theme runs through many of my songs and chants. We need only sufficient certainty to take the next step in our lives and no more. We have, as Christians, some certainties based on our beliefs about Jesus but if we push these to absolute certainties we tip over into fundamentalism of various kinds.

107 Song of the Sun

June Boyce-Tillman (1943–)

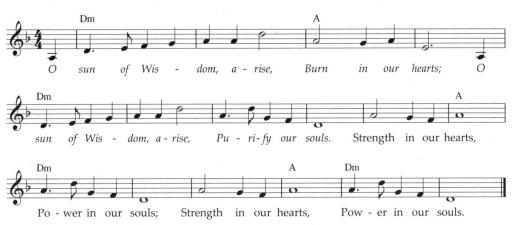

O sun of Wis - dom, a - rise, Burn in our hearts; O
sun of Wis - dom, a - rise, Pu - ri - fy our souls. Strength in our hearts,
Po - wer in our souls; Strength in our hearts, Pow - er in our souls.

O sun of Wisdom, arise,
Burn in our hearts;
O sun of Wisdom, arise,
Purify our souls.

1 Strength in our hearts,
Power in our souls;
Strength in our hearts,
Power in our souls.
Chorus

2 Warmth in our hearts,
Loving in our souls;
Warmth in our hearts,
Loving in our souls.
Chorus

3 Flame in our hearts,
Peace within our souls;
Flame in our hearts,
Peace within our souls.
Chorus

During an ecological celebration of Easter in 2003, at Crystal Spring, Plainville, Massachusetts, I
rose to see the sunrise on Easter morning, and wrote this song. It was sung at that year's summer
solstice, at Cape Cod. It lends itself to the creation of more verses.

108 Hail Full of Grace: A Hymn for Annunciation

June Boyce-Tillman (1943–)

Music © Copyright 2006 Stainer & Bell Ltd

1 O radiance, radiance of morning's new dawn,
 O speak not a word, lest you miss what is born
 From the womb of the Godhead creating with pain,
 The nourishing gifts of the earth's fruit and grain.

2 'Is there one here who is hearing?' God's heartbeat is pleading.
 She is listening, listening, the bread she is kneading,
 The silence enfolds her, deep-hidden its power,
 O daughter, beloved, know this is the hour!

3 O deep is the yearning, for healing she longs,
 For a people's deliverance from oppression and wrongs.
 While moulding the loaf – wheaten flour which earth yields,
 She connects with her sisters still toiling in fields.

4   O daughter, beloved, I heard Rachel's cries
    For the vulnerable children who forever will die.
    Through the violence of culture, my compassion will stream,
    In your waiting, responding, lies my hope and my dream.

5   O strong is the spirit, insistent and wild,
    Evoking response – 'I am Wisdom's child!
    Let my body, my life, as love's gift remain
    For God and my people, for all children in pain.'

6   The silence is broken, there is rushing of wings,
    The cry of the wild goose, exultant it sings –
    'O rise up, daughter, love's power will unfold,
    Revealing the healing of stories untold.'

7   She is rushing through hillside, her sister she seeks,
    In the mutual joy of encounter she speaks:
    'God is listening, hearing, all history's sorrow,
    God is with me, creating, and birthing tomorrow…'

Mary Grey

This setting is of a text by my good friend Mary Grey, Emeritus Professor of Pastoral Theology at the University of Wales, Lampeter, and Professorial and Research Fellow, St Mary's University College, Strawberry Hill, London. It was sung at the 1995 carol service at King Alfred's College, in Mary's presence. It uses powerful images of God as giving birth, which have influenced me a great deal.

109 The Tambourine Woman

WEAVING

June Boyce-Tillman (1943–)

One day as I went out a-walk-ing, A stran-ger ap-peared un-to me. Her skirt was made up of weird pat-ches, A rain-bow in bold ta-pes-try. Silk rib-bons be-gui-ling in co-lour Flowed out from her strange tam-bou-rine. Be-hind her a vast crowd of peo-ple Came leap-ing and sing-ing this theme: We'll

fol - low the tam-bou-rine wo-man   And join in her tam-bou-rine song.   We're

ri-ding a rain-bow to hea-ven   And danc-ing our jour-ney a-long.

1   One day as I went out a-walking,
    A stranger appeared unto me.
    Her skirt was made up of weird patches,
    A rainbow in bold tapestry.
    Silk ribbons beguiling in colour
    Flowed out from her strange tambourine.
    Behind her a vast crowd of people
    Came leaping and singing this theme:
    We'll follow the tambourine woman
    And join in her tambourine song.
    We're riding a rainbow to heaven
    And dancing our journey along.

2   She showed me at first yellow patches,
    The colour of newness and spring,
    Of daffodils, lemon and honey,
    The freshness a new birth can bring.
    But next to them lay the deep purples
    Of mourning, of sadness, of grief,
    Of velvet and softness and richness,
    Of heathers on moorland and heath.
    Chorus

continued overleaf

3 The diamond patches were orange
As rays in the heart of the sun,
Vibrating with warmth and with loving
And speaking of victories won.
But scattered around them were brown ones
That spoke of the healing of earth,
A gentleness, depth and enfolding,
The loving that knows its own worth.
Chorus

4 The reds spoke of magic and anger,
Enchantment, bewitchment and spells,
Of fire that flickers and sparkles,
But also of judgement and hells.
The blues and the greens were much softer
And blended to form a deep lake.
Unfathomable she described it;
We felt we would drown for her sake.
Chorus

5 The song grew in depth and in wideness
And plaited a curious weave
Of colourful tambourine ribbons,
So none of us wanted to leave.
We found we reflected her colours
And singing was making them one –
Our tapestry vibrant with colour
And woven with laughter and fun.
Chorus

In May 1988 I attended a course on discovering your clown, run by Sandra Pollerman, who helped me find my own clowns (see Nos. 104 and 111). Soon after, I wrote this song, partly in response to the course and partly as an attempt to find a feminine version of the popular song of the 1960s entitled 'Mr Tambourine Man'. I have used it as the basis of many Rainbow Days, a school-based project composing pieces based on different colours which are worn together over the session. The symbolism of the colours is drawn from my life-experience. The use of 'WEAVING' as a tune-title reflects what I have learned from the weaver, Evelyn Ross, who has taught me so much about the relationship of weaving to life.

110 Dancing Spirit

June Boyce-Tillman (1943 –)

Ov - er hill and ov - er dell, Tho - rough bush and tho - rough briar,

I go danc - ing ev - ery where, Full of life,— I burn with de - sire.

Over hill and over dell,
Thorough bush and thorough briar,

1 I go dancing everywhere,
Full of life, I burn with desire.
Chorus

2 I am nature's beating heart;
Let my energy set you on fire.
Chorus

3 I will sing a song for you
Filled with music from nature's choir.
Chorus

4 I will lead you in my dance;
In my arms you'll reach up higher.
Chorus

5 With my joy I'll heal your pain,
Forge your strengthening in my fire.
Chorus

6 I will draw you with my love,
Such a loving that can never tire.

This was written as a song for my friend Puck during a retreat led by Penelope Eckersley on Bardsey Island (Ynis Enlli) in 1997. It is based on images of the Holy Spirit calling us to join vigorously in the dance of life.

111   The Holy Fool

Traditional
arranged June Boyce-Tillman (1943–)

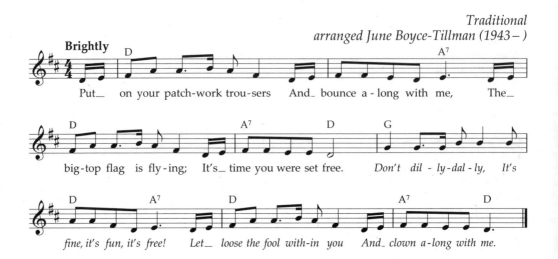

Put_ on your patch-work trou-sers   And_ bounce a-long with me,   The_ big-top flag is fly-ing;   It's_ time you were set free.   Don't dil-ly-dal-ly,   It's fine, it's fun, it's free!   Let_ loose the fool with-in you   And_ clown a-long with me.

2 The band is going 'Oom-pah!'
   And the sawdust circle calls;
   Come, polish up your noses,
   And practise how to fall.
   Chorus

3 Come leaping up the hillside
   With the wounded and the lame;
   A clown will come and touch them;
   They'll never be the same.
   Chorus

4 And now that clown is dying
   Upon a lonely cross;
   Bring all the joy that's in you
   To help you bear that loss.
   Chorus

5 Come dancing in a garden
   To a dark and rocky cave,
   And let your love flow freely
   Where the harlequin is laid.
   Chorus

6 A living, laughing angel
   Calls out, 'He isn't here!
   He's leaping on before you.
   The way to clown is clear.'
   Chorus

7 The circus ring of living
   Will make the wounded whole;
   Put on the boots of loving
   And join the Holy Fool.
   Chorus

I have learned a great deal about Christ and freedom from my clowning with The Holy Fools. I learned about it first from the Rev. Roly Bain who regularly invited me to play as a clown for him – especially at the Big Top in Bognor. This song was written for his Laughter and Healing conference in October 1994 in Salisbury, in gratitude for all that I have discovered from him concerning joy, laughter and the clown as Christ-image.

112 Lullaby

June Boyce-Tillman (1943–)

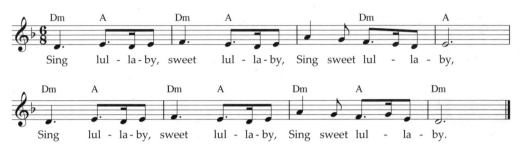

Sing lul-la-by, sweet lul-la-by, Sing sweet lul - la - by,

Sing lul-la-by, sweet lul-la-by, Sing sweet lul - la - by.

1 Sing lullaby, sweet lullaby,
   Sing sweet lullaby,
   Sing lullaby, sweet lullaby,
   Sing sweet lullaby.

2 Sing lullaby, sweet lullaby,
   Rock the soul to rest,
   Sing lullaby, rest lullaby,
   Rest upon God's breast.

3 Sing lullaby, dream lullaby,
   Wounds are healed in sleep,
   Sing lullaby, dream lullaby,
   Let the dreams go deep.

4 Sing lullaby, sleep lullaby,
   Let sweet oil flow,
   Sing lullaby, sleep lullaby,
   Let the wounding go.

5 Sing lullaby, heal lullaby,
   When the wounds are healed,
   Sing lullaby, heal lullaby,
   Scars will be our shield.

6 Sing lullaby, love lullaby,
   Love from God will pour,
   Sing lullaby, love lullaby,
   Joy is born once more.

7 Sing lullaby, sweet lullaby,
   Sing sweet lullaby,
   Sing lullaby, sweet lullaby,
   Sing sweet lullaby.

This was written for a liturgy to heal the wounds of an abortion. We rocked the baby, named it and then blew it away as bubbles in the garden. I have great faith in the power of liturgy to heal, and have written many liturgies of this kind, some of which are in 'Human Rites: Worship Resources for an Age of Change' edited by Hannah Ward and Jennifer Wild (Mowbray/Continuum, 1995).

113 Song for Women's Ordination

Adapted from Personent Hodie by
June Boyce-Tillman (1943–)

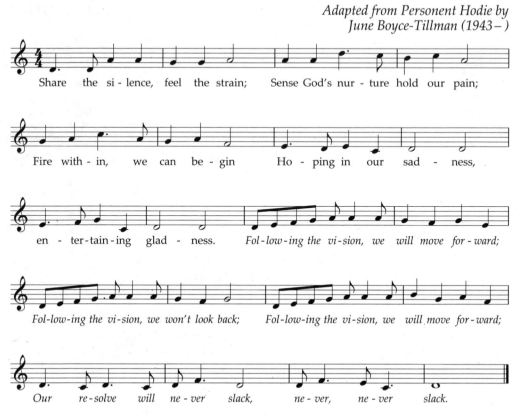

Share the si - lence, feel the strain; Sense God's nur - ture hold our pain;

Fire with - in, we can be - gin Ho - ping in our sad - ness,

en - ter-tain-ing glad - ness. *Fol-low-ing the vi-sion, we will move for-ward;*

Fol-low-ing the vi-sion, we won't look back; Fol-low-ing the vi-sion, we will move for-ward;

Our re-solve will ne - ver slack, ne - ver, ne - ver slack.

1 Share the silence, feel the strain;
Sense God's nurture hold our pain;
Fire within, we can begin
Hoping in our sadness, entertaining gladness.
Following the vision, we will move forward;
Following the vision, we won't look back;
Following the vision, we will move forward
Our resolve will never slack, never, never slack.

2 Share the anger, feel the power
   Make the Spirit in us flower;
   Fire within, we can begin.
   Overcoming weakness, questioning our meekness.
   Chorus

3 Break the silence, voice the shout;
   Use God's strength to end our doubt.
   Fire within, we can begin
   Speaking of our outrage, moving on with courage,
   Chorus

4 Break the bread and lift the cup;
   Now God's joy is lifted up;
   Fire within, we can begin
   Celebrating glory in a woman's story.
   Chorus

This was written for the Women's Ordination Worldwide conference in Ottawa in July 2005. The tune is an adaptation of PERSONENT HODIE with the chorus a version of No. 89. It was sufficiently familiar to be easy to learn. The conference was entitled 'Breaking silence, breaking bread, Christ calls women to lead'. It not only sees women as priests but also redeems women from their position in the writings of some church fathers as flawed men, temptresses and bringers of evil. Here is 'glory in a woman's story'. It was used powerfully on the pre-conference pilgrimage from Washington DC. We sang it remembering Elizabeth Cady Stanton, author of 'The Woman's Bible', Matilda Joslyn Gage, author of 'Woman, Church and State' and Susan B. Anthony at Seneca Falls where the suffragette movement began. Here were women in the nineteenth century linking politics and religion. Accompanied by a drum it marked our entrance into the ring of statues of women (some drinking tea) outside the Parliament buildings in Ottawa. The song was also used for the closing liturgy of the conference organised by my good friend Professor Susan Roll with whom I have often worked liturgically.

114   Song of the Earth

June Boyce-Tillman (1943–)

Sing us our own song, the song of the earth, The song of cre-a-tion, the
song of our birth, That ex-ists in be-long-ing to you and to me, To the
stars and the moun-tains, the sky and the sea. List-en, you're hear-ing the
song of the earth, They sing it who know of their
va-lue and worth, Who know they be-long to the sea and the sky, To the
moon-shine at mid-night, the clouds float-ing by.

2 It is not one song, but patchworks of sound,
   That includes all the pitches that people have found,
   That includes the vibrations of earthquakes and bees,
   Of the laughing fire's crackling and murmuring breeze.
   Chorus

3 All blend together to make the earth song,
   Fragmented parts separated too long,
   In finding our true notes and colours and beats
   We make sacred spaces where we all meet.
   Chorus

Some of my deepest beliefs about the nature of music and its relationship to the earth are encompassed here, in words and music that are rapidly becoming my 'theme song'. I always use my trusty djembe to accompany it – it is a sturdy song that benefits from a drum accompaniment. Dedicated to Veronica Seddon, it is also an important element in my cantata 'The Healing of the Earth'.

115 Angel in my Soul

June Boyce-Tillman (1943–)

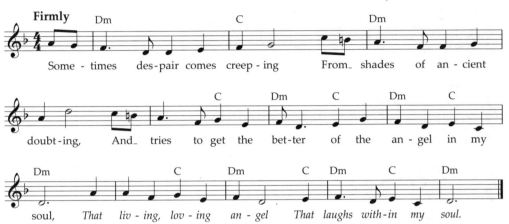

Firmly

Some - times des-pair comes creep - ing From_ shades of an - cient

doubt-ing, And_ tries to get the bet-ter of the an - gel in my

soul, That liv - ing, lov - ing an - gel That laughs with-in my soul.

2 Then I must look around me,
   Within me and beyond me,
   For things that gently will revive
   The angel in my soul,
   Chorus

3 The morning stars at sunrise,
   The river's rapid flowing,
   The natural world – these will embrace
   The angel in my soul,
   Chorus

4 And I must trust the smiling
   Of those whose warmth surrounds me,
   The friends who clearly recognise
   The angel in my soul,
   Chorus

5 For I must go on loving
   In brightness and in shadow
   The joy that is the life-blood of
   The angel in my soul,
   Chorus

In my researches into Hildegard of Bingen I have drawn great strength from the Benedictine Community at the Abtei St Hildegard in Eibingen, Germany. They accepted me and took me to their heart. This song was written during my stay there in 1993 at a seat among the vines called Hildegardis Ruh. It arose from a conversation with Sister Ancilla and was first sung publicly at a gathering at my good friend Lala Winkley's house for Advent in that year. It reflects my lifelong struggle with depression.

116   The Wounds that Weep

June Boyce-Tillman (1943–)

1   The smile is faultless, the colours vibrant,
   The voice is powerful and strong,
   The shoes are polished, the walking measured,
   And the eyes look straight and long.
   But underneath it the wounds are crying,
   But underneath it they weep,
   But underneath it the wounds are sighing
   For the cuts are wide and deep.

2   The earth is greening, the heather blooming,
   The snails are gliding along,
   The stones are sparkling, the peaks are glistening,
   And the birds joy in their song.
   Chorus

3   The desk is polished, the marble glistens,
   The hall is spotless and gleams,
   The voices murmur, the suits are tailored
   And a well-dressed woman cleans.
   Chorus

4   The systems sparkle, the wheels are oiled,
    The managers' moves are clear,
    And change moves swiftly, and all seems ordered
    And the staff have good careers.
    Chorus

5   The church is towering, the pews are straightened,
    The knees are bending and kneel;
    The choir sings softly, the coins fall clinking,
    And the preacher wants to heal.
    Chorus

6   How are we missing the signs of weeping?
    Will there be some who protest?
    And is there loving to tend the wounded
    And a healing place of rest?
    For underneath it the wounds are crying,
    For underneath it they weep,
    For underneath it the wounds are sighing
    For the cuts are wide and deep.

I began this song after hearing the story of a woman who carried on her professional life efficiently and capably while undergoing the last of a series of IVF treatments, all of which were unsuccessful. Verse four is based on my own experience of very rapid, poorly managed change in one of my workplaces. Verse five reflects many women's experience of churches of every denomination.

117 A Song for the Assumption

June Boyce-Tillman (1943–)

There are times when we catch the e-cho Of the part-ies in heaven a-bove, And we

long to join the danc-ing To the band of Ce-lest-ial Love; so let's go

Bounc-ing to hea-ven with Ma - ry,   *Bounc-ing to hea-ven with Ma - ry,*
Bounc-ing our way__ to hea - ven,   *Bounc-ing our way__ to hea - ven,*

Bounc-ing to hea-ven with Ma - ry To dance with the ang - el clowns.
Bounc-ing our way__ to hea - ven To dance with the ang - el clowns.

© Copyright 2006 Stainer & Bell Ltd

1 There are times when we catch the echo
   Of the parties in heaven above,
   And we long to join the dancing
   To the band of Celestial Love; so let's go
   Bouncing to heaven with Mary,
   Bouncing to heaven with Mary,
   Bouncing to heaven with Mary
   To dance with the angel clowns.

2 The doors stand wide in welcome,
   The streets are cushioned air;
   The angels will do massage,
   To relax newcomers there; so join us
   Chorus

3 The heavenly choir sings gladly
   In a worship jamboree;
   The children leap in pleasure
   For the angel rides are free; so they are
   Chorus

4 The wine is flowing freely
   As we trample the olive press,
   And no one is excluded from
   The domestic happiness; when we go
   Chorus

5 At night the sleep is dreamless
   And the stars will always shine;
   The angels sing in harmony;
   Their Schubert is divine, as we go
   Chorus

6 So put on your fashion trainers
   And jog along with me,
   For it's not too far to the pearly gates
   And we're in good company, when we are
   Chorus

Alternative chorus:

   Bouncing our way to heaven,
   Bouncing our way to heaven,
   Bouncing our way to heaven
   To dance with the angel clowns.

I wrote this song by the swimming pool at Prasada, in August 2001, after visiting a church with an amazing statue of the Virgin Mary sitting on a blue cloud that looked like a bouncy castle. In May 2004 I adapted the song as an alternative for more general use by adding another chorus.

118 The Story Tree

June Boyce-Tillman (1943–)

There stood in hea-ven a lin-den tree Whose leaves_ would heal_ the na - tions, Of ma - ny co - lours, ma - ny shapes And each con - tained_ a sto - ry. We'll tell the sto - ries that heal the earth, Heal the earth, heal the earth, We'll tell the sto-ries that heal the earth And help_ it to_ re - birth._

For Brigitta

1 There stood in heaven a linden tree
Whose leaves would heal the nations,
Of many colours, many shapes
And each contained a story.
We'll tell the stories that heal the earth,
Heal the earth, heal the earth,
We'll tell the stories that heal the earth
And help it to rebirth.

2 Some stories fell as binding rope
   To keep the people tightly bound
   With laws and morals and beliefs.
   These stories had not hope.
   Chorus

3 Sometimes the leaves would fall as tears
   And freeze in people's grieving hearts
   As daggers, swords and sharpened spears
   And stories full of tears.
   Chorus

4 But some oozed love and warming fire
   And melted people's frozen lives
   Like those of Brigid's welcoming home
   Where tended flames leapt high.
   Chorus

5 Then children did not recognise
   The words for gun or cluster bomb.
   'They're from our past,' the elders said,
   'We see with different eyes.'
   Chorus

This was written to celebrate Brigitta Löwe's D.Min at the Episcopal Divinity School, Cambridge, Massachusetts, USA in 2003. It celebrates her work on children's stories and the role that stories play in our lives. My time as Proctor Scholar at the Divinity School, initiated by Professor Kwok Pui Lan, was a transformative time for me. My one-woman performances tell lost women's stories. Brigitta showed how stories have a powerful influence on us, especially in childhood. It is a shame that the media do not tell the peace stories as often as they do the war stories.

119   Connection

The chorus is to be accompanied by claps on the first three crotchets of each bar.

1   The air is blowing everywhere
    And serving all the earth;
    Come, flowing air,
    Flow free and pure.
    For the rock is connected with the sea
    And the sea is connected with the air,
    And the air is the link joining all the human race
    With the wolf and the lamb and the bear.

2   There's loving at the heart of earth,
    Compassion for us all,
    Mysterious flame,
    Infuse our hearts.
    Chorus

A seventieth-birthday present for Ianthe Pratt in 1999, this was used at her 'croning' ceremony at the Julie Billiart Centre. This is a ceremony we do as a group of women when one of us reaches seventy. The crone is given a cloak and shares her wisdom with us. It was enjoyed by the children in the cantata 'The Healing of the Earth'. It is based on Hildegard's antiphon 'Aer enim volat'.

120 Song for the Jubilee

June Boyce-Tillman (1943–)

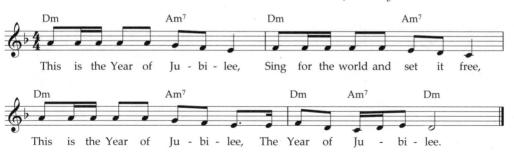

This is the Year of Ju - bi - lee, Sing for the world and set it free,

This is the Year of Ju - bi - lee, The Year of Ju - bi - lee.

1 This is the Year of Jubilee,
   Sing for the world and set it free,
   This is the Year of Jubilee,
   The Year of Jubilee.

2 This is the Year of Jubilee,
   Weep for the world and set it free,
   This is the Year of Jubilee,
   The Year of Jubilee.

3 This is the Year of Jubilee,
   Bind up the wounds, set people free,
   This is the Year of Jubilee,
   The Year of Jubilee.

4 This is the Year of Jubilee,
   Cancel the debts, set people free,
   This is the Year of Jubilee,
   The Year of Jubilee.

5 This is the Year of Jubilee,
   Strengthen the weak and set them free,
   This is the Year of Jubilee,
   The Year of Jubilee.

When the G8 summit was held in Birmingham in 2000, I wrote this song for the Jubilee 2000 campaign that marched through the city and formed a human chain around the conference centre where the meetings were scheduled to take place. It was an amazing experience, with dancing and instruments, and a great spirit, when the circle was complete, of having made a statement about breaking the chain of poverty and abuse of the poor by the rich.

121 Roots

Traditional North American Lullaby

Trees stand firm,   roots reach down, Ground - ed   in the earth's deep warm - ing.

For Carol

1 Trees stand firm, roots reach down,
   Grounded in the earth's deep warming.

2 Branch and leaf stretching out
   Draw their Wisdom from connecting.

3 We abide in that love
   Firmly found in human friendship.

4 We can stand unafraid
   Rooted in a God incarnate.

5 Homeless Christ, form our roots,
   So our branches blossom freely.

This song, written as a birthday present for Carol Boulter, was part of my Christmas letter of 1996. While working as a Reader in Community and Performing Arts at King Alfred's, Winchester, I have lived in a caravan parked in the New Forest. This was a way of exploring my own roots in this area where I was brought up. I have found the strengthening power of the trees here and have also contacted some of my 'lost' relations who still live in the forest area. It draws on experiences of snow weighing down the trees on the road from Fordingbridge to Cadnam. It has taken me a long time to find my real roots and I have been something of a wanderer geographically, psychologically and spiritually. It is through good friendships that I started to feel a sense of belonging. The strengthening power of these is for me a place of the incarnation of the Divine in our world. Carol has been an important part of my supportive network of friends. I met her through Womenchurch, Reading, and have been a regular visitor who has been warmly welcomed in her home. The text is set to a traditional lullaby tune, 'All the pretty little horses'.

122 A Duan of Barra

June Boyce-Tillman (1943–)

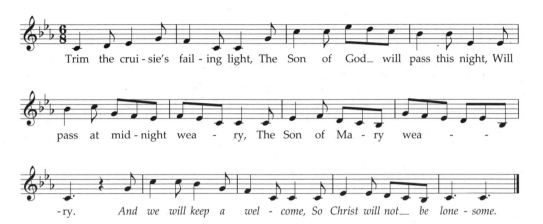

Trim the crui-sie's fail-ing light, The Son of God_ will pass this night, Will pass at mid-night wea - ry, The Son of Ma - ry wea - - -ry. And we will keep a wel - come, So Christ will not_ be lone - some.

To Demetra and Stergios

1 Trim the cruisie's failing light,
   The Son of God will pass this night,
   Will pass at midnight weary,
   The Son of Mary weary.
   And we will keep a welcome,
   So Christ will not be lonesome.

2 Lift the sneck and wooden bar,
   And leave the stranger's door ajar,
   Lest he may tarry lowly,
   The Son of Mary holy.
   Chorus

3 Sweep the heart and pile the peat,
   And set the board with bread and meat;
   The Son of God may take it,
   The Son of Mary break it.
   Chorus

I wrote this in Thessaloniki with the friends to whom it is dedicated, in October 2005. They made me so welcome, especially with a wonderful agape near Mount Olympus. The text is an adaptation of a traditional Hebridean source. I used it in a sermon at St Paul's, Furzedown on God's hospitality.

123 Strong Women

June Boyce-Tillman (1943–)

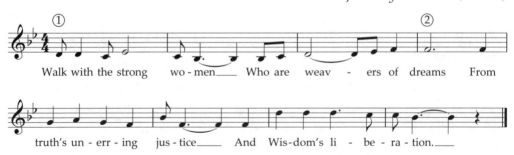

Walk with the strong wo-men____ Who are weav - ers of dreams From

truth's un - err - ing jus - tice____ And Wis-dom's li - be - ra - tion.____

This is a two-part round.

For Professor Lisa Isherwood

1 Walk with the strong women
  Who are weavers of dreams
  From truth's unerring justice
  And Wisdom's liberation.

2 Work with the strong women
  Who are weavers of dreams
  From truth's unerring justice
  And Wisdom's liberation.

3 Weep with the strong women
  Who are weavers of dreams
  From truth's unerring justice
  And Wisdom's liberation.

4 Stand with the strong women
  Who are weavers of dreams
  From truth's unerring justice
  And Wisdom's liberation.

5 Pray with the strong women
  Who are weavers of dreams
  From truth's unerring justice
  And Wisdom's liberation.

6 Laugh with the strong women
  Who are weavers of dreams
  From truth's unerring justice
  And Wisdom's liberation.

7 Dance with the strong women
  Who are weavers of dreams
  From truth's unerring justice
  And Wisdom's liberation.

This was written to celebrate Lisa Isherwood's Professorship in Feminist Liberation Theology at the College of St Mark and St John, Plymouth in 2003. There are a number of songs (see Nos. 125 and 126) reworking this theme. Lisa has been a good friend and in organising the Britain and Ireland School of Feminist Theology and editing the journal 'Feminist Theology' (Sage Publications) and series of books making feminist theology more widely available, has been a significant disseminator of feminist ideas. She has supported and affirmed many women on their journeys.

124 We are the Body of Christ

June Boyce-Tillman (1943–)

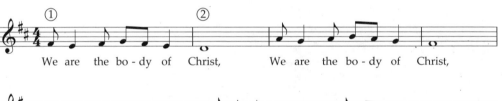

We are the bo-dy of Christ, We are the bo-dy of Christ,

We are the bo-dy, Weav-ing to-ge-ther, We are the bo-dy of Christ.

This is a two-part round.

1 We are the body of Christ,
We are the body of Christ,
We are the body,
Weaving together,
We are the body of Christ.

2 We are the body of Christ,
We are the body of Christ,
We are the body,
Sharing together,
We are the body of Christ.

3 We are the body of Christ,
We are the body of Christ,
We are the body,
Battered and broken,
We are the body of Christ.

4 We are the body of Christ,
We are the body of Christ,
We are the body,
Rising together,
We are the body of Christ.

5 We are the body of Christ,
We are the body of Christ,
We are the body,
Living together,
We are the body of Christ.

Words and Music © Copyright 2006 Stainer & Bell Ltd

This was the core song of an Easter celebration at Holy Rood House, using the arts to bring the story alive. On Maundy Thursday we made a great patchwork skirt of Christ showing how we are all joined together in community (verses one and two). On Good Friday we cut it up and looked at the scattered fragments on the chapel floor. It was a devastating experience. We had destroyed the beautiful thing we had made (verse three). The fragments were hidden round the garden and on Easter Saturday we searched for them and stitched them back together, and the garment with its 'wounds' showing formed part of the Easter Sunday sunrise liturgy (verse four). On Easter Monday we pitched it like a tent and talked about dwelling in Christ (verse five).

125   Wise Women

June Boyce-Tillman (1943–)

We are the Wise Wo-men And the sing - ers of songs;

We are the Wise Wo-men And we dance and we laugh.

This can be sung as a four-part round.

1 We are the Wise Women
   And the singers of songs;
   We are the Wise Women
   And we dance and we laugh.

2 We are the Wise Women
   And the healers of wounds;
   We are the Wise Women
   And we weep and anoint.

3 We are the Wise Women
   And the tellers of tales;
   We are the Wise Women
   We remember, reshape.

4 We are the Wise Women
   And the earth is our root;
   We are the Wise Women
   And we grow firm and strong.

5 We are the Wise Women
   And the weavers of dreams;
   We are the Wise Women
   And we love and we trust.

This was written for Emma Winkley's 18th birthday in 1998. Emma is Lala and Austin's daughter and a lively young feminist who has enriched the life of the Catholic Women's Network.

126 Wise Women

June Boyce-Tillman (1943–)

We are the Wise Wo-men And we chal - lenge the world.

We are the Wise Wo-men And we hope and we act.

This can be sung as a four-part round.

1 We are the Wise Women
   And we challenge the world.
   We are the Wise Women
   And we hope and we act.

2 We are the Wise Women
   And our presence is strong.
   We are the Wise Women
   And we hope and we act.

3 We are the Wise Women
   And we're called to be priests.
   We are the Wise Women
   And we hope and we act.

In 1998 the Rev. Jean Mayland organised a gathering in Durham to mark the end of the Ecumenical Decade – Churches in Solidarity with Women. It was a UK and Ireland conference and took place in the College of St Hild and St Bede in April of that year. There was a splendid event in Durham Cathedral on the Saturday night at which I sang Hildegard chants in the Galilee Chapel. The Sunday Eucharist included one of the many uses of 'We shall go out with hope of resurrection'. I adapted No. 125 for this gathering, introducing the notion of priesthood for women.

127 The Lighting of the Candles

June Boyce-Tillman (1943–)

We light the can - dles here With all th'an-ge - lic host, With
A - ri - el__ the one In form the love - li - est, With U - ri - el__ of
my - stic charms In heav'n's__ high courts The shin - ing one.

1 We light the candles here
With all the angelic host,
With Ariel the one
In form the loveliest,
With Uriel of mystic charms
In heaven's high courts
The shining one.

2 We light the candles here
Without malicious thoughts,
Without a jealous heart,
Or envy, fear or hate.
No terror here
Of anyone beneath the sun
Or living shades.

3 May God the holy One,
Shield us from every harm,
Free us from jealousy
Or envy, fear or hate,
Keep terror far
Of anyone beneath the sun
Or living shades.

4 O Holy Spirit's fire,
Now kindle love within,
For foes, for friends, for kin,
The brave, the bound, the free.
O holy flame,
Your love extends from lowliest depths
To highest realms.

This text, based on a Celtic source, may also be sung to DARWALL'S 148TH. This tune was written for a creative liturgy using Celtic themes in February 2005 at St James's, Piccadilly. The text links the candles with the angels. I have become very interested in the place of angels in contemporary Christian thinking. Angels are found in most world faiths and figure highly in New Age thinking. I have a strong sense of their presence, especially at the Eucharist (see No. 102). The Rt Rev. Professor Elizabeth Stuart (see No. 96) tells me that the dismissal 'Go in peace' is to the angels, who will always gather at this most sacred feast.

128   Hymn for Bernard of Clairvaux

June Boyce-Tillman (1943–)

Chorus

2 When we are fearful, She will protect us from all harm,
   When She is steering gently without weariness we will land;
   And She is just the aqueduct through which all grace can flow
   As She holds us in the hollow of Her hand.
   Chorus

I adapted this at Prasada, Montauroux – on the Feast of St Bernard of Clairvaux in 2001 – from a Hymn to the Virgin by Bernard. For Hildegard, his contemporary, Wisdom and the Virgin Mary were closely linked. Mary incarnates Wisdom as does Jesus.

Prayer, Protest, Power

June Boyce-Tillman (1943–)

We weave our dreams of li - be - ra - tion,
Wo - ven with pro - test,___ li - tur - gy and prayer, To
con - tra - dict po - ver - ty___ and a - li - en - a - tion, With Ju - lie and Fran - çoise,
Ma - ry Woll - sten - craft, E - li - za - beth Ca - dy Stan - ton, E -
-li - za - beth Schuss - ler Fio - ren - za, Ur - su - la King, Do - ro - the - a Mc -
Ew - an, And My - ra and all of us to - ge - ther. We will act u - pon our
call. Be - neath these la - bour - ing dreams we strug - gle; Be -
-neath these la - bour - ing dreams we're strong; Be - neath these la - bour - ing dreams we
rise a - gain, Peo - ple of pro - test, pow - er and song.

For Myra

1 We weave our dreams of liberation,
    Woven with protest, liturgy and prayer,
    To contradict poverty and alienation,
          With Julie and Françoise,
          Mary Wollstencraft,
          Elizabeth Cady Stanton,
          Elizabeth Schussler Fiorenza,
          Ursula King,
          Dorothea McEwan,
    And Myra and all of us together.
    We will act upon our call.
    Beneath these labouring dreams we struggle;
    Beneath these labouring dreams we're strong;
    Beneath these labouring dreams we rise again,
    People of protest, power and song.

2 We weave our dreams in contemplation,
    Woven in chaos, struggle and despair.
    With authority we challenge crude normalisations,
          With Julie and Françoise,
          Hildegard and Julian,
          Teresa of Avila,
          Luce Iragaray,
          Edwina Gately,
          Grace Jantzen,
    And Myra and all of us together.
    We will act upon our call.
    Chorus

3 We weave our justice-seeking friendships,
    Communities of passion, stubborn in resistance;
    And these survival spaces challenge dictatorships,
          With Julie and Françoise,
          Elizabeth Stuart,
          Mary Hunt,
          John McCarthy,
          Brian Keenan,
          Sally McFague,
    And Myra and all of us together.
    We will act upon our call.
    Chorus

continued overleaf

4　We trust that suffering is redemptive,
　　Rooted in the cross in liminal space,
　　To eliminate structures as they grow more oppressive,
　　　　With Julie and Françoise,
　　　　Chung Hyun Kyung,
　　　　Sally Purvis,
　　　　Mary Grey,
　　　　Julia Kristeva,
　　　　Aruna Gnanadason,
　　And Myra and all of us together.
　　We will act upon our call.
　　Chorus

5　We weave our dreams of revolution,
　　Woven on the threshold from visions of change.
　　We draw on Julie's charism that the good God is very good,
　　　　With Julie and Françoise,
　　　　Mary St Philip,
　　　　Susan O'Brien,
　　　　Pope John the twenty-third,
　　　　Rosemary Radford Ruether,
　　　　Joan Chittester,
　　And Myra and all of us together.
　　We will act upon our call.
　　Chorus

This was written in 2001 to celebrate Myra Poole's book 'Prayer, Protest, Power: The Spirituality of Julie Billiart Today' (Canterbury Press, 2001) and draws upon the people mentioned in it. It uses a structure like the English song 'Widdecombe Fair'. It sees the powerful link between dreams and social action as witnessed in the lives of great mystics like Julie Billiart, founder of the Sisters of Notre Dame. Myra contemporises her story.

130 What Will You Leave Behind?

June Boyce-Tillman (1943–)

What will you find at the end of your living days
In the trunk at the end of the bed
When your eyelids close?
I would leave behind for my family and friends
And the world to which I belong
Only tokens of my love.

This incomplete song celebrates our dying and asks about our legacy. It was written in 2003 as part of a project to write a Requiem, which is still unfinished, although I moved it forward when I was on a placement with the local undertaker as part of my ordination training. Many of us at some time must turn out our parents' house, and this song reflects on the emotional strain it can entail.

131 Friendship

June Boyce-Tillman (1943–)

When you're far from home And your hope is gone, Hope is gone,
hope is gone, My strength will be there, My strength will
verses 1-5 | *Last time*
be there, I will car-ry you. | be there, I am your friend.

1 When you're far from home
   And your hope is gone,
   Hope is gone, hope is gone,
   My strength will be there,
   My strength will be there,
   I will carry you.

2 In your shuttered fear
   Where the memories hide,
   Memories hide, memories hide,
   My courage will be there,
   My courage will be there,
   I will carry you.

3 In the face of hate
   When the fists are clenched,
   Fists are clenched, fists are clenched,
   My love will be there,
   My love will be there,
   I will carry you.

4 In the sharpening pain
   Where the bone spears bite,
   Bone spears bite, bone spears bite,
   My ointment will be there,
   My ointment will be there,
   I will carry you.

5 At the time of death
   When the eyelids close,
   Eyelids close, eyelids close,
   My comfort will be there,
   My comfort will be there,
   I will carry you.

6 In your going out
   And your coming in,
   Going out, coming in,
   I'll always be there,
   I'll always be there,
   I am your friend.

This was written for the millennial party of Elizabeth and Stanley Baxter celebrating how Holy Rood House, Centre for Health and Pastoral Theology is there for so many vulnerable people. I wrote it in one of the little books which are in each room and contain the experiences of people who have stayed in them. The rooms have names like Creativity, Adventure and Peace. It was sung memorably at a garden Eucharist celebrated by Archbishop David Hope. It also forms the 'death' sequence in the performance 'Lunacy or the Pursuit of the Goddess'.

132   Resurrection Wisdom

June Boyce-Tillman (1943–)

Wo-men in a boat, fish-ing for hope, Fish-ing for hope, in the
long dark night. Catch a glimpse of Wis-dom in the wa-ters be-low,
Scin-til-lat-ing sil-ver in the half-moon light. Re-sur-rec-tion morn-ing,
Re-sur-rec-tion song, Re-sur-rec-tion glo-ry, The place where we be-long.

For Dorothea

1   Women in a boat, fishing for hope,
     Fishing for hope, in the long dark night.
     Catch a glimpse of Wisdom in the waters below,
     Scintillating silver in the half-moon light.
     Resurrection morning,
     Resurrection song,
     Resurrection glory,
     The place where we belong.

2   Women on a picnic, playing for joy,
     Playing for joy in the waves at play.
     Catch a glimpse of glory on the high seashore,
     Resurrection Wisdom in the sunlit day.
     Chorus

This was written for a celebration of Dorothea McEwan's birthday as a picnic in Hyde Park in May 2001. Dorothea has been very significant in her contribution to the dissemination of feminist theological thought, for example by editing liturgical collections of material by women such as 'Making Liturgy: Creating Rituals for Worship and Life' (Canterbury Press, 2001). This publication, co-edited with my good friends Pat Pinsent, Ianthe Pratt and Veronica Seddon, contains much material from these alternative liturgies.

133 Identity

June Boyce-Tillman (1943–)

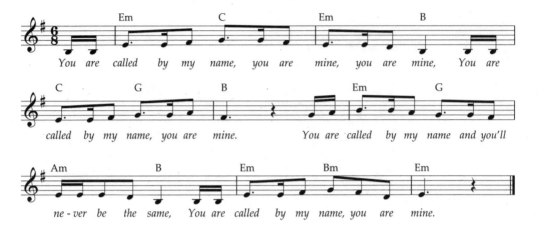

For Bronwen and Ian

You are called by my name, you are mine, you are mine,
You are called by my name, you are mine.
You are called by my name and you'll never be the same,
You are called by my name, you are mine.

1   As we look at our past with its pain and its joy,
    And we ponder the future with dread,
    In our hearts we will find there's a love that's undestroyed
    And a whispering voice in our ear.
    Chorus

2   We can search for our truth in the scholarly texts
    And seek for our loving from friends,
    But inside in a mirror we find that we reflect
    The image of love that God sends.
    Chorus

3   We manoeuvre the hills and the vales in our selves
    And wonder about our own worth;
    Yet inside we will find in our bodies' deepest cells
    The song that was sung at our birth.
    Chorus

Verse and chorus use the same tune in this song, which was written in November 2005 and is based on Isaiah. It relates to the experience and the chorus text of No. 90. Bronwen managed the rebirthing experience and the Rev. Canon Ian Ainsworth-Smith (see No. 53) was alongside me here as he has been in many difficult experiences in my life.

Chants

If my hymns occupy that domain where the private yields to the public, and if my songs reverse that formula, then the chants bear strongly on my experience of meditation practices involving mantras, influenced by the Fellowship of Contemplative Prayer.

These chants in their various styles and forms have suffused much of my work, and versions of them can be found, for example, in my Hildegard presentations. Musically, many of them use repeated chord patterns, so they can be vehicles for improvisation. Spiritually, being more circular structures, they allow the word of God to dwell inside; and where the actual form of the round is used, by allowing different things to happen simultaneously yet in a way that fits together, they become a wonderful metaphor for world peace.

134   God's Generosity

June Boyce-Tillman (1943–)

A - maz-ing grace, a - maz-ing grace, Hope for the groan-ing earth; A -
-maz-ing grace, a - maz-ing grace, Joy in the green-ing power.

This is a four-part round.

1 Amazing grace, amazing grace,
   Hope for the groaning earth;
   Amazing grace, amazing grace,
   Joy in the greening power.

2 Amazing grace, amazing grace,
   Hope for the hungry poor;
   Amazing grace, amazing grace,
   Thanks for the greening power.

3 Amazing grace, amazing grace,
   Alleluia.
   Amazing grace, amazing grace,
   Alleluia.

This was a commission for the wonderful Easter celebrated by Catholic Women's Network at Noddfa retreat centre in Penmaenmawr, North Wales in 2004. Their gatherings are always a time of transformation, to which we all contribute. This was written for the amazing Easter breakfast following our sunrise liturgy on the mountains overlooking the sea.

135   Ave Maris Stella

June Boyce-Tillman (1943–)

A - ve ma - ris stel - la, De - i Ma - ter al - ma,

At - que sem-per Vir - go Fe - lix cae - li por - ta. A - men.

Music © Copyright 2006 Stainer & Bell Ltd

1 Ave maris stella,
   Dei Mater alma,
   Atque semper Virgo,
   Felix caeli porta.

2 Sumens illud Ave
   Gabriélis ore,
   Funda nos in pace,
   Mutans Hevae nomen.

3 Solve vincla reis,
   Profer lumen caecis,
   Mala nostra pelle,
   Bona cuncta posce.

4 Monstra te esse matrem,
   Sumat per te preces,
   Qui pro nobis natus
   Tulit esse tuus.

5 Virgo singuláris,
   Inter omnes mitis,
   Nos culpis solútos
   Mites fac et castos.
   Amen.

Eighth-century Latin

As a Protestant, I came freshly to Mary (see Nos. 36 and 37). I love this image of Mary as 'star of the sea' – stella maris. The piece was written in 2002 as a submission to the festival celebrating St Bridget of Sweden's birth 700 years earlier in Rome (see No. 156). This was entitled 'For a Better and More Just World: The Way of Beauty'. It included Lutheran women priests alongside Roman Catholic cardinals – an amazing experience. The festival was organised by Donne in Musica and my good friend Patricia Adkins Chiti who has done so much for Women in Music. At this conference she suggested that the Vatican liturgical committee should include three women.

136 Come, Holy Spirit

June Boyce-Tillman (1943–)

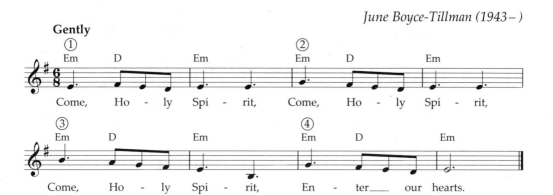

Gently

Come, Holy Spirit, Come, Holy Spirit, Come, Holy Spirit, En-ter our hearts.

This is a four-part round based on Em and D chords.

1 Come, Holy Spirit,
  Come, Holy Spirit,
  Come, Holy Spirit,
  Enter our hearts.

2 Come, strengthening Spirit,
  Come, strengthening Spirit,
  Come, strengthening Spirit,
  Enter our hearts.

3 Come, loving Spirit,
  Come, loving Spirit,
  Come, loving Spirit,
  Enter our hearts.

4 Come, dancing Spirit,
  Come, dancing Spirit,
  Come, dancing Spirit,
  Enter our hearts.

Words and Music © Copyright 2006 Stainer & Bell Ltd

This chant and No. 137 were written for the Catholic Women's Ordination walking around the piazza of Westminster Cathedral, which they carry out every first Wednesday in the month. Repeated, it seems to have charismatic power.

137 Come, Spirit, Circle Us

June Boyce-Tillman (1943–)

Slowly

Come, Spi-rit, cir-cle us, Keep love with-in E-vil out-side.

Words and Music © Copyright 2006 Stainer & Bell Ltd

This chant, a six-part round, and No. 136 were used at the Hildegard group at my house that met from 1992 to 1994 to make music.

138 Christ is our Peace

June Boyce-Tillman (1943–)

© Copyright 2006 Stainer & Bell Ltd

1 Christ is our peace,
  Making us whole,
  Rooted in love,
  We grow.
  Christ is our peace,
  Making us whole,
  Rooted in love,
  We grow.
  Christ is our peace,
  Making us whole,
  Rooted in love,
  We grow.

2 Christ nôtre paix,
  Nous guérissant,
  Nous grandissons
  D'amour.
  Christ nôtre paix,
  Nous guérissant,
  Nous grandissons
  D'amour.
  Christ nôtre paix,
  Nous guérissant,
  Nous grandissons
  D'amour.

3 Christus Friede,
  Mache uns ganz,
  Wir in der Lieb,
  Wachsen.
  Christus Friede,
  Mache uns ganz,
  Wir in der Lieb,
  Wachsen.
  Christus Friede,
  Mache uns ganz,
  Wir in der Lieb,
  Wachsen.

This was commissioned as the theme song of the gathering of the Ecumenical Forum of the European Christian Women in York in July 1989, which explains the three languages. It is based on a repeated chord sequence, and therefore can be used for groups of singers to improvise over, in the manner of Taizé chants like 'Veni, Sancte Spiritus'. The tune is dedicated to Penelope Eckersley, who has helped me to stay rooted in love and to transform some of the most difficult parts of my past, for example with a ritual bonfire in her garden. This piece was used at EXPO 2000 in Hannover.

39   Come, Sophia Wisdom

June Boyce-Tillman (1943–)

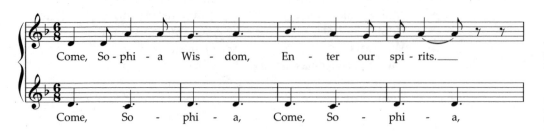

Come, So-phi - a Wis - dom,   En - ter   our   spi - rits.___

Come,   So -   phi - a,   Come,   So -   phi - a,

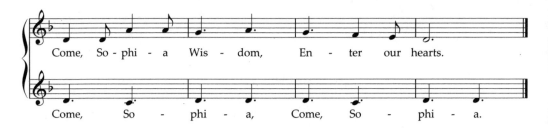

Come, So-phi - a Wis - dom,   En - ter   our   hearts.

Come,   So -   phi - a,   Come,   So -   phi - a.

1 Come, Sophia Wisdom,
   Enter our spirits.
   Come, Sophia Wisdom,
   Enter our hearts.

2 Come, Sophia Wisdom,
   Enter our bodies.
   Come, Sophia Wisdom,
   Enter our souls.

Words and Music © Copyright 2006 Stainer & Bell Ltd

This was written in 2005 for a Wisdom Eucharist I planned as part of my ordination course. It also features in my cantata 'Peacesong', first performed in Winchester Cathedral on 4 March 2006.

140   Come, Spirit of God

June Boyce-Tillman (1943–)

①   ②   ③

Come,   Spi - rit   of   God,   Come,   Spi - rit   of   God,

                     ④

Come,   Spi - rit   of   God,   En - ter___   our   hearts.

Words and Music © Copyright 2006 Stainer & Bell Ltd

A responsory to a biblical reading, this was written for a liturgy on the Southwark Diocese Ordained Local Ministry course in 2003.

141   Mystery

June Boyce-Tillman (1943–)

God of an - swers,   God_ of ques - tions,   Dwell_____ in__ our lives.

We would know you,   We__would not   know,   Dwell_____ in__ our lives.

God of answers,
God of questions,
Dwell in our lives.
We would know you,
We would not know,
Dwell in our lives.

This chant was written at the same time as No. 34 for a liturgy in the doctrine module of my ordination course. It reflects the danger of too much certainty in our faith, leading to arrogance.

142   Hear Our Prayer

June Boyce-Tillman (1943–)

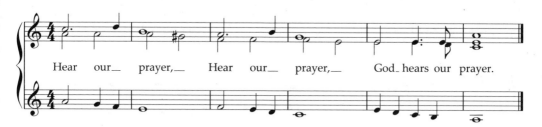

Hear   our_   prayer,__   Hear   our_   prayer,__   God_ hears our   prayer.

Hear our prayer,
Hear our prayer,
God hears our prayer.

This simple chant is regularly used for the intercessions at St Paul's, Furzedown, where John Mitchell, the organist, and the Revs. John and Janet Driver have been so supportive of my preparation for ordination. It was used in my cantata 'A Greening Branch' first performed at the Church Choirs Festival in the Arts Centre, Twickenham. The piece is based on Hildegard's 'Hymn to the Virgin'.

143   Passover Chant

June Boyce-Tillman (1943–)

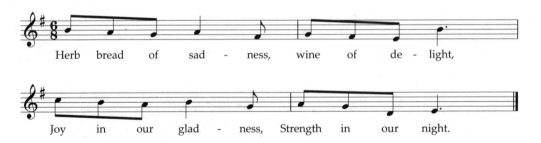

Herb bread of sad - ness, wine of de - light,

Joy in our glad - ness, Strength in our night.

Words and Music © Copyright 2006 Stainer & Bell Ltd

This was created for the Seder meal at Ianthe Pratt's house on 8 April 2006 at the beginning of Holy Week. Ianthe and her late husband Oliver played a significant part in the development of home liturgies, from the 1960s onwards.

144   Grace for a Meal

Adapted from Personent Hodie by
June Boyce-Tillman (1943–)

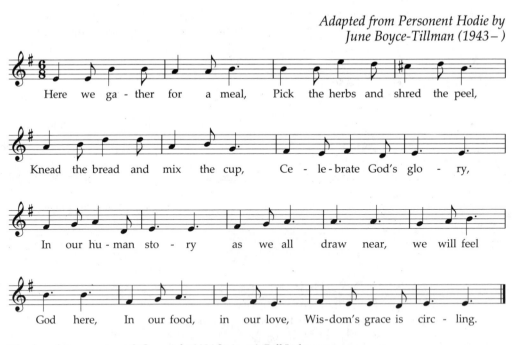

Here we ga - ther for a meal, Pick the herbs and shred the peel,

Knead the bread and mix the cup, Ce - le - brate God's glo - ry,

In our hu - man sto - ry as we all draw near, we will feel

God here, In our food, in our love, Wis-dom's grace is circ - ling.

Words and Arrangement © Copyright 2006 Stainer & Bell Ltd

This was created for but not sung at the Seder meal at Ianthe Pratt's house, 8 April 2006. It was first sung at Women Word Spirit Easter at Noddfa, 17 April 2006, for Maundy Thursday. This was an Easter celebration that we created around the theme of 'Who rolled the stone away?', and we looked at the stones that needed rolling away in our lives, such as sexism, racism and elitism.

145   Hold Fast to the Earth

June Boyce-Tillman (1943–)

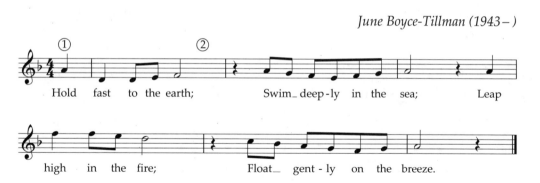

Hold fast to the earth; Swim deep-ly in the sea; Leap

high in the fire; Float gent-ly on the breeze.

Words and Music © Copyright 2006 Stainer & Bell Ltd

In my Christmas letters I always include a song or a poem, or both, and this two-part round was the contribution for 1999. It was also included in my cantata finished for the Queen's Golden Jubilee in 2002, 'The Healing of the Earth' (see No. 114).

146   Sanctus and Benedictus

June Boyce-Tillman (1943–)

Strongly

Ho - ly, ho - ly, ho - ly, Lord
Bless - ed, bless - ed, bless - ed, Bless - ed

God of· Hosts, Heaven and earth are
is the one Com - ing in the

full of your glo - ry. Ho - san - na in the high - est.
name of the Lord.

Music © Copyright 2006 Stainer & Bell Ltd

For a garden Eucharist at the house of my good friend, Ianthe Pratt, I wrote this short chant in 1994. It has been sung regularly in her garden since then. It is a beautiful liturgy with many people present from different backgrounds. The birds sing and the plants and shrubs grow profusely. We do the intercessions using the flowers to remember people. It is a real eco-Eucharist in which we feel a connection with the natural world as well as each other. In this liturgy, as in many feminist liturgies, there is ample time to debate and discuss our ideas and experiences. The piece is led by a cantor, with the congregation repeating the phrase.

147 Confidence in Quietness

June Boyce-Tillman (1943–)

Gently

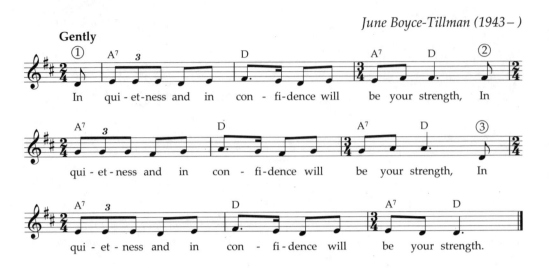

In qui-et-ness and in con-fi-dence will be your strength, In
qui-et-ness and in con-fi-dence will be your strength, In
qui-et-ness and in con-fi-dence will be your strength.

Words and Music © Copyright 2006 Stainer & Bell Ltd

A three-part round based on the chords A⁷ and D. This reflects my own meditation practice and its centrality to my prayer life (see Introduction).

148 Resurrection Song

June Boyce-Tillman (1943–)

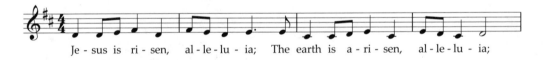

Je-sus is ri-sen, al-le-lu-ia; The earth is a-ri-sen, al-le-lu-ia;

We are a-ri-sen, al-le-lu-ia, Al-le-lu-ia, al-le-lu-ia.

> Jesus is risen, alleluia;
> The earth is risen, alleluia;
> We are arisen, alleluia,
> Alleluia, alleluia.

Words and Music © Copyright 2006 Stainer & Bell Ltd

For the Catholic Women's Network's Easter celebrations at Noddfa in 2004 I wrote this chant on the theme of the empty tomb. We danced to it round the garden of this beautiful retreat house run by Mary Jo and Patrice SSHH, who have been such good companions on my journey.

149 Agnus Dei

June Boyce-Tillman (1943–)

Lamb_ of God, *Lamb_ of God,* You take_ a-way, *You take_ a-way* the sin of__ the world,___ *The sin of__ the world,___* Have mer-cy on us, Have mer-cy on us. *Have mer-cy on us, Have mer-cy on us.* Lamb_ of God, *Lamb_ of God,* You take_ a-way, *You take_ a-way* the sin of__ the world,___ *The sin of__ the world,___* Grant us___ peace,_ peace,_ *Grant us___ peace,_ peace._*

For Ianthe

Lamb of God,
Lamb of God,
You take away,
You take away the sin of the world,
The sin of the world,
Have mercy on us,
Have mercy on us.
Have mercy on us,
Have mercy on us.

Lamb of God,
Lamb of God,
You take away,
You take away the sin of the world,
The sin of the world,
Grant us peace, peace,
Grant us peace, peace.

This was written for Ianthe Pratt's garden Eucharist in July 2004. It is designed to be led by a cantor, whose phrases are repeated by the congregation (text in italics).

150   Hymn from Philippians

Philippians 2: 5-11 (NRSV)   *June Boyce-Tillman (1943–)*

Let the same mind be __ in you _____ that was in Christ Je - sus who, though he was

in the form _ of God,   did not re-gard e - qua -li - ty with God   as some-thing to be ex -

-ploi - ted,   but emp - - tied him-self, tak-ing the form of a slave,   be -

- ing born in hu - man like-ness, And be-ing found in hu - man form,   he

hum - - bled him-self _____ And be-came o - be - - di-ent

to the point of death   e - ven a death _____ on   a cross.

There-fore God al - so high-ly ex - al - ted him   and gave _____ him the __

name   that is a-bove ev'-ry name   so that at the name of Je - - sus

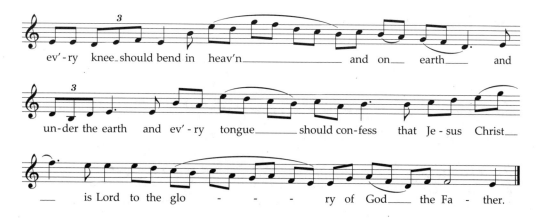

> ev'-ry knee should bend in heav'n _____ and on __ earth ___ and under the earth and ev'-ry tongue _____ should con-fess that Je - sus Christ ___ is Lord to the glo - - - ry of God ___ the Fa - ther.

There are some passages in the New Testament that were certainly hymns in the early church. This is one of them and I set it for a carol service at King Alfred's College of Higher Education in 2002 at the suggestion of the Rev. Jonathan Watkins, who has encouraged many of my creative projects. The chant owes a great deal to my singing of Hildegard's chants, and uses the phrygian mode, which was one of her favourites. The chant may be divided between two voices in performance.

151   Christ Within

June Boyce-Tillman (1943–)

> Late have I found you, Christ with - in; Now will I love you, Christ with - in; Of - fer you my heart, Christ with - in; For it is your heart, Christ in all cre - a - tion.

Late have I found you, Christ within;
Now will I love you, Christ within;
Offer you my heart, Christ within;
For it is your heart, Christ in all creation.

This was written at a point on my journey when I found an inner authority. It has proved to chime in with many women's experiences later in their life.

152   Magnificat

The Book of Common Prayer, 1662   June Boyce-Tillman (1943–)

hun-gry with good__ things and the rich he__ hath__ sent emp - ty__

__ a - way. He re-mem-bering his__ mer - cy hath hol-pen his

ser - vant Is - ra - el as he pro-mised to our fore - fa - thers,

A - bra - ham and his seed, for - e - - - ver.

For many years I sang in the choir of St Mary's, Southampton, and was married there. I wrote this Magnificat in the 1950s, when I was asked for a setting in simple folk-like style that Mary might have sung. I sang it high in the organ loft while Mary danced below.

153 Magnificat

June Boyce-Tillman (1943–)

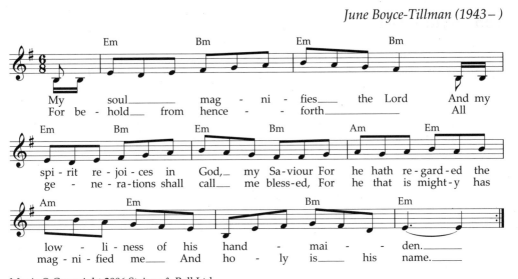

My soul__ mag - ni - fies__ the Lord And my
For be - hold__ from hence - - forth__ All

spi - rit re - joi - ces in God,__ my Sa-viour For he hath re - gard-ed the
ge - ne - ra-tions shall call__ me bless-ed, For he that is might-y has

low - li - ness of his hand - mai - - den.__
mag - ni - fied me__ And ho - ly is__ his name.__

Music © Copyright 2006 Stainer & Bell Ltd

This was written in the 1970s for a nativity presentation in St Paul's, Furzedown. It was sung by Esther Himmel as Mary. The text is deliberately simple but can be easily adapted to the Book of Common Prayer version by substituting 'doth magnify' and 'hath rejoiced'. I had hoped to use No. 152 but had lost the copy and had to write a new version very quickly.

154 Kyrie

Gently

June Boyce-Tillman (1943–)

① Lord, have mer-cy, Lord, have mer-cy, Lord, have mer - cy,

② Christ, have mer-cy, Christ, have mer-cy, Christ, have mer - cy,

③ Lord, have mer - cy, Lord, have mer - cy.

Text from *Common Worship: Services and Prayers for the Church of England* (Church House Publishing, 2000), © Copyright 1988 English Language Liturgical Consultation. Reproduced by permission of the publisher. Music © Copyright 2006 Stainer & Bell Ltd

A three-part round based on Em D Em B (the opening sequence of 'Greensleeves').

155 Nunc Dimittis

The Book of Common Prayer, 1662

June Boyce-Tillman (1943–)

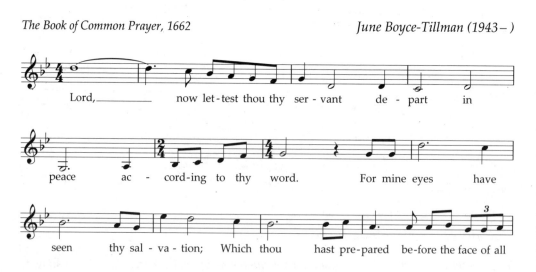

Lord,_____ now let-test thou thy ser - vant de - part in

peace ac - cord-ing to thy word. For mine eyes have

seen thy sal - va - tion; Which thou hast pre-pared be-fore the face of all

Extracts from The Book of Common Prayer, the rights in which are vested in the Crown, are reproduced by permission of the Crown's Patentee, Cambridge University Press. Music © Copyright 2006 Stainer & Bell Ltd

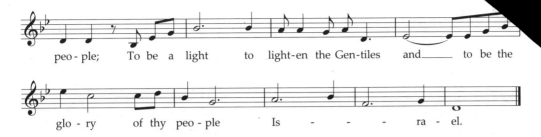

peo - ple; To be a light to light-en the Gen-tiles and___ to be the glo - ry of thy peo - ple Is - - - ra - el.

I was asked to lead a taster session for sixth-formers who might want to read theology at university in 2002. I chose a mixture of song and story and wrote this as part of it.

156　Gaude Birgitta

June Boyce-Tillman (1943–)

Ro - sa, ro - rans bo - ni - ta - tem, Stel - la stil - lans cla - ri - ta - tem, Bir - git - ta, vas gra - ti - ae.

Music © Copyright 2006 Stainer & Bell Ltd

1　Rosa, rorans bonitatem,
　Stella stillans claritatem,
　Birgitta, vas gratiae.

2　Rora coeli pietatem,
　Stilla vitae puritatem
　In vallem miseriae.

3　Christus ductor, dulcis doctor,
　Te dilexit te direxit
　In aetate tenera.

4　Tuque mitis, virens vitis
　Profecesti et crevisti
　Florens super sidera.

5　Mentens mundans, fidem fundans
　Amor cinxit et te vinxit
　In sancto proposito.

6　Tota decens tota recens
　Christum amas, Christus clamans
　Toto vitae stadium.

Medieval Latin Hymn

Like my setting of Ave Maris Stella (No. 135), this was written for a festival celebrating the life of St Bridget. It was sung at the opening on 4 October 2002, in the Palazzo della Cancelloria in the Vatican by the Coro de Fiorentini.

egard Rounds

June Boyce-Tillman (1943 –)

Like fea-thers are we blown, beau-ti-ful-ly blown,

beau-ti-ful-ly blown on the breath of God. Like fea-thers are we blown,

beau-ti-ful-ly blown Gent-ly are we car-ried on the breath of God.

Per - fume of ho-li-ness, in-fuse our souls,

Flow___ through the u - ni - verse, mak - ing it whole.

The cir-cle of God___ is sur-round-ing the u-ni-verse,

Roll-ing us, en-fold-ing us in life - giv-ing truth.

Me - lo - dy of God's grace___ shape us;

Rhy-thm of God make us strong; Har-mo-ny of God

bring re-so-lu-tion; Then with Wis-dom's voice will we sing.

Run your hands— a-cross the strings of our— lives;— Play—— the
notes———— that you wish to play. We can-not sound un-less you
fill us with love. Then will we re-so-nate in Wis-dom's way.

This set of rounds was written to go in the one-woman performance 'Singing the Mystery: Hildegard of Bingen'. They were written on a plane going to Austin, Texas, where I was to do a performance for the Hildegard Community. This was an amazing experience of a community working out a really communal spiritual life based on inclusive and ecological views of what church should be. The first four are rounds. The fifth is based on a Hildegard chant.

158   Rubens Rosa

Medieval Latin Hymn   *June Boyce-Tillman (1943–)*

Meditatively

Ru - bens Ro - sa, tunc— pal-lu-it Dum— na - ti mor-tem do-lu-it
Ru - bens Ro - sa, Ru - bens Ro - sa,

Vir - go, quem vox pro-phe - ti-ca Di-xit pas-su - ru ta-li-a.
Ru - bens Ro - sa, Ru - bens Ro - sa.

Music © Copyright 2006 Stainer & Bell Ltd

It is envisaged that the choir will sing the upper line and the congregation the lower ones. It is designed to be sung as a meditation. This, like Nos. 135 and 156 was written for the St Bridget celebrations in Rome in 2002. The text refers to the Virgin Mary as a rose, an image that has been very important to me.

159 Sophia

June Boyce-Tillman (1943 –)

Fast and energetic (like a Bulgarian dance)

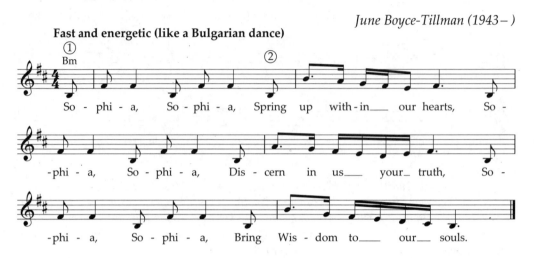

So - phi - a, So - phi - a, Spring up with-in___ our hearts, So -
-phi - a, So - phi - a, Dis - cern in us___ your_ truth, So -
-phi - a, So - phi - a, Bring Wis - dom to___ our_ souls.

Words and Music © Copyright 2006 Stainer & Bell Ltd

This simple chant, for which I had the style of a Bulgarian dance in mind, is dedicated to Professor Mary Grey to whose work on Sophia I owe a great deal. It was first sung at one of her lectures at St James's, Piccadilly in 1994. It has formed part of several of my longer pieces, including the music theatre piece on Hildegard, 'A Life Apart'.

160 Walk Softly

June Boyce-Tillman (1943 –)

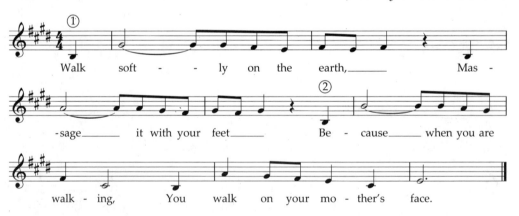

Walk soft - - ly on the earth,___ Mas -
-sage___ it with your feet___ Be - cause___ when you are
walk - ing, You walk on your mo - ther's face.

Words and Music © Copyright 2006 Stainer & Bell Ltd

This simple two-part round is taken from the words of the theologian Chung Hyun Kyung, whom I met at the women's festival in Harare, Zimbabwe in November 1998, where she performed a healing ritual after a moving session on the abuse of women. It is part of my one-woman show 'Lunacy or the Pursuit of the Goddess' and my cantata 'The Healing of the Earth'. The last line always comes as a great surprise. My good friend Helen Arundel used this chant very effectively in the walking of the labyrinth that she constructed from fragments of memorabilia as part of her art course.

161 Greening Power Grace

June Boyce-Tillman (1943–)

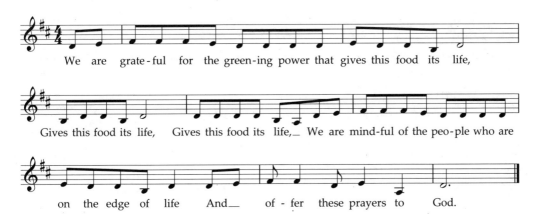

We are grate-ful for the green-ing power that gives this food its life,

Gives this food its life, Gives this food its life,— We are mind-ful of the peo-ple who are

on the edge of life And— of-fer these prayers to God.

This was written for Holy Rood House in 2001. It draws on the notion of the greening power that gives life to everything, and how this is passed to us through the food we eat.

162 Labyrinth Song

June Boyce-Tillman (1943–)

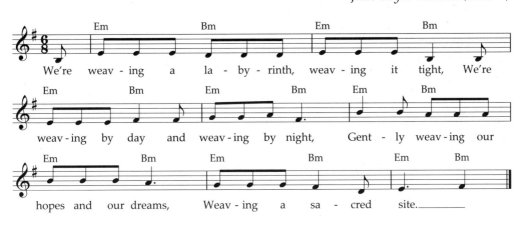

Em   Bm   Em   Bm

We're weav-ing a la-by-rinth, weav-ing it tight, We're

Em   Bm   Em   Bm   Em   Bm

weav-ing by day and weav-ing by night, Gent-ly weav-ing our

Em   Bm   Em   Bm   Em   Bm

hopes and our dreams, Weav-ing a sa-cred site._____

The labyrinth is a timeless image and for many people today its symbolism is a powerful contemplative tool. The use of repetitive chords is designed to induce the reflective atmosphere. This was designed to accompany a labyrinth meditation such as the one led by the Catholic priest Dana Reynolds in Chartres in October 2006. I helped to play for the ordination of Dana and a number of other women on the river at Gananoque. It was an amazing experience of joy and power. We all laid hands on these holy women in a silence broken only by the lap of the water on the boat and the song of the birds.

163 Grace

June Boyce-Tillman (1943–)

We give thanks, we give thanks, we give thanks For the
e - ner - gy of sun and moon and earth. We give thanks, we give thanks, we give
thanks_____ For hu - man hands that bring us to new birth.

We give thanks, we give thanks, we give thanks
For the energy of sun and moon and earth.
We give thanks, we give thanks, we give thanks
For human hands that bring us to new birth.

Written for Holy Rood House in 1998, this grace is designed to give thanks for both the natural world and the support of human beings.

164 Easter Round

June Boyce-Tillman (1943–)

Wip-ing, weep-ing, watch-ing, wit-ness-ing, We are wait-ing for the dawn.

Wiping, weeping, watching, witnessing,
We are waiting for the dawn.

I wrote this round for the Catholic Women's Easter celebrations held at Twickenham in 2000 led by Lala Winkley and Veronica Seddon. The music is based on a Hebrew round, and the words reflect the progress of the group through the Easter story seen by the eyes of the women. We sang it powerfully in Bushey Park at sunrise on Easter morning much to the surprise of early-morning dog walkers!

165 Weaving Wisdom's Circle

June Boyce-Tillman (1943–)

Words and Music © Copyright 2006 Stainer & Bell Ltd

This was written for the European Women's Synod in Gmunden, Austria, 1999 and hence the variety of languages. When we sang it one of the participants said it sounded like heaven. The round structure means that the different languages overlap with one another and still the piece makes sense.

166   The Good Life

June Boyce-Tillman (1943–)

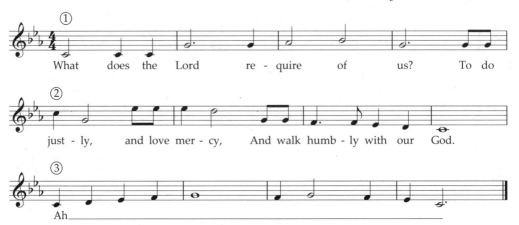

① What does the Lord re - quire of us? To do

② just - ly, and love mer - cy, And walk humb - ly with our God.

③ Ah_____

A round based on Micah 6, which is a very special text for me as it was preached at my father's funeral and summarises the life of this gentle, upright, faithful man superbly.

167   Feather on the Breath of God

> With the living spirit we're going,
> Feather on the breath of God;
> With the living spirit we're going,
> Feather on the breath of God;
> With the living spirit we would go,
> Feather on the breath of God.

This meditative chant, sung to the tune PICARDY, is central to my one-woman performance 'Singing the Mystery – Hildegard of Bingen'. In this chant, different images of God are substituted for 'feather on the breath of God'. Some of these are:

> *Harp within the hands of God*
> *Gold within the flame of God*
> *Arc within the wheel of God*
> *Warmth within the kiss of God*
> *Phrase within the song of God*
> *Scent within the perfume of God*
> *Drop within the fountain of God*

It is also used in my opera based on Hildegard: 'A Life Apart – Hildegard of Bingen', recorded by Elizabeth Glen and John Beswick on the CD 'Singing the Mystery: Hildegard Revisited'. Here it is sung to the chant PANGE LINGUA GLORIOSA.

Index of First Lines

(First lines of choruses are shown in italics)

203

Index of Titles